Cross-linguistic Similarity
in Foreign Language Learning

PEFC

PEFC/16-33-111

CATG-PEFC-052

www.pefc.org

SECOND LANGUAGE ACQUISITION
Series Editor: Professor David Singleton *Trinity College, Dublin, Ireland*

This series brings together titles dealing with a variety of aspects of language acquisition and processing in situations where a language or languages other than the native language is involved. Second language is thus interpreted in its broadest possible sense. The volumes included in the series all offer in their different ways, on the one hand, exposition and discussion of empirical findings and, on the other, some degree of theoretical reflection. In this latter connection, no particular theoretical stance is privileged in the series; nor is any relevant perspective – sociolinguistic, psycholinguistic, neurolinguistic, etc. – deemed out of place. The intended readership of the series includes final-year undergraduates working on second language acquisition projects, postgraduate students involved in second language acquisition research, and researchers and teachers in general whose interests include a second language acquisition component.

Other Books in the Series
Age, Accent and Experience in Second Language Acquisition
  Alene Moyer
Studying Speaking to Inform Second Language Learning
  Diana Boxer and Andrew D. Cohen (eds)
Language Acquisition: The Age Factor (2nd edn)
  David Singleton and Lisa Ryan
Focus on French as a Foreign Language: Multidisciplinary Approaches
  Jean-Marc Dewaele (ed.)
Second Language Writing Systems
  Vivian Cook and Benedetta Bassetti (eds)
Third Language Learners: Pragmatic Production and Awareness
  Maria Pilar Safont Jordà
Artificial Intelligence in Second Language Learning: Raising Error Awareness
  Marina Dodigovic
Studies of Fossilization in Second Language Acquisition
  ZhaoHong Han and Terence Odlin (eds)
Language Learners in Study Abroad Contexts
  Margaret A. DuFon and Eton Churchill (eds)
Early Trilingualism: A Focus on Questions
  Julia D. Barnes
Cross-linguistic Influences in the Second Language Lexicon
  Janusz Arabski (ed.)
Motivation, Language Attitudes and Globalisation: A Hungarian Perspective
  Zoltán Dörnyei, Kata Csizér and Nóra Németh
Age and the Rate of Foreign Language Learning
  Carmen Muñoz (ed.)
Investigating Tasks in Formal Language Learning
  María del Pilar García Mayo (ed.)
Input for Instructed L2 Learners: The Relevance of Relevance
  Anna Nizegorodcew

For more details of these or any other of our publications, please contact:
Multilingual Matters, Frankfurt Lodge, Clevedon Hall,
Victoria Road, Clevedon, BS21 7HH, England
http://www.multilingual-matters.com

SECOND LANGUAGE ACQUISITION 21
Series Editor: David Singleton, *Trinity College, Dublin, Ireland*

Cross-linguistic Similarity in Foreign Language Learning

Håkan Ringbom

MULTILINGUAL MATTERS LTD
Clevedon • Buffalo • Toronto

Library of Congress Cataloging in Publication Data
Ringbom, Håkan.
Cross-linguistic Similarity in Foreign Language Learning/Hakan Ringbom.
Second Language Acquisition: 21
Includes bibliographical references and index.
1. Language and languages–Study and teaching. 2. Similarity (Language learning)
I. Title.
P53.777.R56 2007
418.001'9–dc22   2006022410

British Library Cataloguing in Publication Data
A catalogue entry for this book is available from the British Library.

ISBN-13: 978-1-85359-935-4 (hbk)
ISBN-13: 978-1-85359-934-7 (pbk)

Multilingual Matters Ltd
UK: Frankfurt Lodge, Clevedon Hall, Victoria Road, Clevedon BS21 7HH.
USA: UTP, 2250 Military Road, Tonawanda, NY 14150, USA.
Canada: UTP, 5201 Dufferin Street, North York, Ontario M3H 5T8, Canada.

The policy of Multilingual Matters/Channel View Publications is to use papers that are natural, renewable and recyclable products, made from wood grown in sustainable forests. In the manufacturing process of our books, and to further support our policy, preference is given to printers that have FSC and PEFC Chain of Custody accreditation. The FSC and/or PEFC logos will appear on those books where full accreditation has been granted to the printer concerned.

Typeset by Wordworks Ltd.
Printed and bound in Great Britain by MPG Books Ltd.

Contents

Acknowledgements

Scott Jarvis has provided helpful comments on this manuscript. Some sections have been read and commented on by Frank Daulton, Britta Hufeisen and Kalevi Pohjala. I am very grateful for all this help.

For financial assistance with travel grants, I thank The Finnish Society for Sciences and Letters and the H.W. Donner Trust (Åbo Akademi Foundation).

Chapter 1
Introduction

Learning, including language learning, is based on prior knowledge. When you learn something new, such as a foreign language, you try to connect the new elements to whatever linguistic and other knowledge you may have. Both intralinguistic and cross-linguistic knowledge are relevant to the learner of another language. The relevance of intralinguistic TL (target language) knowledge largely depends on the stage of learning: it increases as learning progresses. How relevant prior cross-linguistic knowledge is primarily depends on the relationships that can be established between the TL and L1 (first language). If you learn a language closely related to your L1, prior knowledge will be consistently useful, but if the languages are very distant, not much prior knowledge is relevant. What matters to the language learner is language proximity, i.e. similarities, not its negative counterpart, language distance, i.e. differences. Presence or absence of cross-linguistic similarities accounts for the differences in effort and time existing between learning a language close to the L1 and learning a totally unrelated language.

While language learners are primarily concerned with what similarities they can establish between TL and L1 or any other language they already know, linguists have tended to focus on analysing differences between languages and uses of language. Variability is a key concept in various linguistic contexts, as de Saussure already noted in his statement '*Dans la langue il n'y a que des différences*'. It is certainly true that 'the study of SLA requires an understanding of variation and the nature of the constraints on variable systems over time' (Romaine, 2003: 431). When research has focused upon similarities across languages, the idea has more often than not been to pave the way for a totally different area of theoretical linguistic studies, that of language universals. But the learner's point of view differs from that of the researcher. Learners, consciously or not, do not look for differences, they look for similarities wherever they can find them. In their search for ways of facilitating their learning task they make use of intra-lingual similarities, which are perceived from what they have already learned of the TL. At early stages of learning, when the TL knowledge is insignificant, L1 is the main source for perceiving linguistic similarities, but languages other than the L1 may also play an important part. Many previous studies, especially of Asian or African learners learning English or French, have shown that learners rely on their knowledge of an L2 (second language) related to the TL much more than on their unrelated L1. Perceiving and making use of cross-linguistic similarities to existing linguistic knowledge is important in the learner's striving to facilitate the learning task. L1 and other languages known to the learner clearly provide an essential aid, not a troublesome obstacle for learning a new language. As, for example, Hall says (2002: 81), we often underestimate how much learners bring to the learning task. Ausubel's motto for his 1968 book is worth quoting: 'If I had to reduce all of educational psychology to just one principle, I would say this: The most important single factor influencing learning is what the learner already knows. Ascertain this and teach him accordingly'. Neuner (1992: 158) makes the same point: 'It is a general and basic law of any kind of learning that we associate new elements, items and structures with elements, items and structures already stored in our memory'.

The use of cross-linguistic similarities, i.e. transfer, is an integral part of how people learn languages. It can be manifested in various ways, and we need to study these in depth. There is a fair amount of literature on transfer, but the scope of transfer studies needs to be widened. Transfer has mostly been discussed in connection with Error Analysis, where learners' L1-based deviations (especially syntactic ones) from the norm of the TL have been easy to spot, while the ways in which L1-knowledge has facilitated learning are much more difficult to notice. Material so far provided mainly by errors should, however, be used for assessing the underlying processes in different circumstances, taking into account how the perception of similarities affect learning. In SLA (second language acquisition) research, the process of learning has been almost wholly seen as learning for production.

One of the aims of this book is to argue that the concept of second/foreign language learning should be split up into two distinct types of learning: learning for comprehension and learning for production. If comprehension has been discussed at all in SLA research, the three concepts of comprehension, learning and production have rarely been kept sufficiently distinct. There are obvious differences between comprehension and production. We may have learnt to understand a language reasonably well, yet cannot speak or write it. The retrieval mechanisms are simply different. It is not enough to say that we merely need practice to convert our receptive knowledge into productive knowledge: what we need in order to produce the foreign language is to learn to use the underlying mechanism of target language production, and all that this entails. Practice, of course, is one, but not the only, necessary component in this process. The mechanism of production is different from the one we learnt for comprehending the language, and clear manifestations of the differences are provided by how learners use cross-linguistic similarities. In vocabulary studies similarities have been found to be relevant when cognates have been studied, but this topic needs to be seen in relation to other areas in which learners make use of cross-linguistic similarities. Vocabulary acquisition and grammatical studies, which have often been pursued as isolated branches of investigation, need to be brought into closer contact with each other. The different ways in which transfer is manifested in comprehension and production and in the various linguistic areas should be set out more comprehensively than has been done so far.

This study seeks to elucidate the manifold aspects of cross-linguistic similarities and the learner's use of them in comprehension, in learning (both learning for comprehension and learning for production) and in production. The interaction of transfer with other variables in SLA is, however, complex and many more approaches originating from associated linguistic and psychological disciplines are needed to provide a full picture of exactly how similarities, cross-linguistic as well as intralinguistic, affect the learning of a new language.

Most tests of English surveyed in this study have been given to learners in Finland, which is a country exceptionally well suited for comparative investigations of foreign language learning because of the cultural and educational unity of Finnish and Swedish speakers in the country (see below, pp. 34ff.).

This book is a further development of ideas briefly put forward in my previous book from 1987 and some later articles (Ringbom, 1992, 2005, 2006). It opens with an outline of the different types of cross-linguistic similarities. Chapter 3 deals with L2 comprehension, a relatively neglected area in SLA research. It begins with a survey of some research into comprehension of an unfamiliar language and further describes the language situation in Scandinavia, where speakers of Swedish, Norwegian and Danish can use their own L1 and rely on being generally understood in the neighbour countries. The next two chapters focus on the differences in the use of cross-linguistic similarities in comprehension and production and outline the language situation in present-day Finland. In Chapter 6 the results of various tests of English in Finland are analysed, comparing Finnish and Swedish speakers. Chapters 7 and 8 provide a discussion of how two different types of transfer, item transfer and procedural transfer, are manifested in learner language. The concepts of skill theory and automaticity are briefly commented upon in Chapter 9. Chapter 10 is an account of how foreign language learning develops, beginning with item learning for comprehension and ending with system learning for production, with the intermediate stages of item learning for production and system learning for comprehension. The last chapters before the conclusion sketch possible consequences for language teaching, and the need for further research.

A subsidiary aim of this book is to provide a survey of research in the learning of English in Finland, making use of available national statistics and also taking into account a comparative international perspective. Information will be given on some relatively unknown Finnish works dealing with transfer-related aspects of foreign language learning in Finland.

Chapter 2

Different Types of Cross-linguistic Similarities

Similarity, Contrast and Zero Relations

Similarity is basic, difference secondary. The search for similarities is an essential process in learning. The natural procedure in learning something new is to establish a relation between a new proposition or task and what already exists in the mind. Chronologically, perception of similarity, something positive, comes first, differences, something negative, come into the picture only if similarities cannot be established. Noordman-Vonk (1979: 51): also has a relevant comment: 'When subjects have to judge whether a certain relation between concepts exists, they first try to find positive evidence for that relation. If this cannot be found, they will try to find evidence that falsifies the relation'. Semantic similarity is thus judged at an earlier stage of the process than semantic difference. Schachter (1983: 102) agrees: 'Normal adults ... tend to look for verification of their hypotheses, not disconfirmation'. We do not establish negative relations until we are sure a positive relation does not exist. However, in order to establish meaningful differences there must be an underlying similarity. As Corder (1973: 234) says, 'In order to compare anything the dimensions or categories used must be applicable to both objects'. James (1980: 169) makes the same point: 'It is only against a background of sameness that differences are significant'. Making use of perceived cross-linguistic as well as intralinguistic similarities facilitates the learning task.

As in all semantic matters, there is no sharp borderline between difference and similarity. They are in different positions on a continuum, where we can discern three cross-linguistic similarity relations: (1) a similarity relation, (2) a contrast relation, and (3) a zero relation.

The similarity relation means that an item or pattern in the TL is perceived as formally and/or functionally similar to a form or pattern in L1 or some other language known to the learner. A natural tendency in learners, especially at early stages of learning, is trying to establish a one-to-one relationship with a unit in another language, usually the L1. 'Word usage in a second language was shown to be strongly influenced by a *semantic equivalence hypothesis* which presumes that conceptual patterns and linguistic coding practices in the L1 provide the essential criteria for those in the L2' (Ijaz, 1986: 448; see also, for example, Biskup, 1992; Hasselgren, 1994). Across related languages there will be cognates similar in both form and meaning. Full-scale cross-linguistic similarity of both form and function is, however, rare, except for very closely related languages such as Swedish and Norwegian, which in principle are mutually comprehensible. If there is grammatical congruence, this means fewer problems for the learner. An English learner will find that the noun morphology of Swedish works in much the same way as in his L1: there are only two cases, nominative and genitive. Establishing cross-linguistic similarity relations is particularly relevant for the comprehension of a new language. When both formal and functional similarities can be established, this makes for positive transfer.

Germanic and Romance languages do not generally stand in either a similarity or a zero relation to each other: they tend to have contrast relations. In a contrast relation (cf. James, 1998: 179) the learner perceives a TL item or pattern as in important ways differing from an L1 form or pattern, though there is also an underlying similarity between them. The English learner who is used to a specific third-person ending of the present tense of verbs will notice that German has a host of other personal endings for the verb as well. This means that there are problems for the learner in producing correct verbs forms, but the learner is basically aware of the existence of a system and does not have to expend great effort on learning to understand the functions of endings. Native speakers of English learning a Germanic or Romance target language will encounter both similarities and differences in varying proportions. In other words, there is both positive and negative transfer, but only negative transfer is immediately visible to the researcher. Exactly how differences relate to underlying similarities and to what extent their effect is facilitative or inhibitive is a complex question that needs to be worked out for each individual language relation. As Duskova (1984: 113) says, factors other than merely linguistic ones are also relevant here.

The zero relation does not mean that the learner finds nothing at all that is relevant to L1 as the learning progresses. There are, after all, some linguistic universals common to all languages. But the level of abstraction in these universals is so high that an average language learner cannot easily notice features that a totally different TL has in common with L1. The zero relation merely means that items and patterns in the TL at early stages of learning appear to have little or no perceptible relation to the L1 or any other language the learner knows. The learner's L1 may lack the concepts necessary to perceive fundamental distinctions in the TL. For one thing, it takes time to understand the details of a totally different TL writing system. The learner starts learning from a platform considerably lower than the starting point for a learner who can relate at least some basic features to elements in L1. A learner who knows only Indo-European languages and starts learning Chinese will find it difficult to relate anything to his previous linguistic knowledge. The zero, or near-zero, relation of Chinese to English poses great difficulties at the early stages of learning. As Singley and Anderson say (1989: 114), 'the worst possible transfer situation is when there is no overlap between two sets of productions, in which case transfer is zero, not negative.' The learner has to spend considerable time figuring out how the new language really works. The magnitude of the learning task 'largely corresponds to the formal linguistic relatedness of the languages in question to the mother tongue' (Corder, 1979: 28). A non-Indo-European language, even if it is using the Roman alphabet, also poses initial problems, as clear similarities are not very easy to notice. Even if a closer inspection may reveal a few parallels (such as the existence of loan-words), lexical similarities tend to refer to low-frequency words not encountered at early stages of learning. Where structural similarities can be found across wholly unrelated languages, they normally need to be pointed out to the learner in an explicit way.

Perceived and 'Objective' Similarity

Kellerman stated in his seminal 1977 paper that cross-linguistic similarity relates to what the learner *perceives* to be similar between the target language and another language, usually the L1. It is not the same as 'objective' similarity. Two attempts to define objective cross-linguistic similarity theoretically are Ard & Homburg (1983: 165ff.), where parameters of form and meaning are set out,[1] and Ellegård, 1978. The criteria used for this have varied, and none of the suggested definitions has made a visible impact on SLA research. Still, it *might* be possible to arrive at a generally accepted procedure to measure language similarity. If such objective cross-linguistic similarity could be established, it would be symmetrical. Perceived similarity, on the other hand, is not necessarily symmetrical, i.e. going both ways, and in this respect it behaves like the related concept of intelligibility. Speakers of language X may find it easier to understand language Y than speakers of language Y to understand language X. Perceived similarity is a fuzzy concept, which may be elucidated if the various ways and the various circumstances in which it is manifested are studied. It is broader in scope and has more variation compared with the similarity analysed by the linguist. It is also more difficult to grasp, as it brings in the dimension of individual learner variation. The term *psychotypology* has been applied to the perception of proximity/distance between languages, but there are certainly problems when it comes 'to make precise what the criteria are for determining similarity or equivalence' (Eckman, 2004: 517).

It is obvious that a target language related to L1 is perceived to be at least in some respects similar, while an unrelated language provides little concrete material for tentative cross-linguistic identification. Hall & Ecke (2005) studied the attitudes of multilingual learners who knew English and Spanish and were studying German and French. More than 80% judged English to be easier for a Spanish speaker and more than 90% thought German was easier to learn than Spanish for an English speaker. Genetic relatedness overlaps with perceived similarity, though in principle the two concepts should be distinguished. It is possible to perceive at least some similarities also across wholly unrelated languages, and all aspects of a related target language can hardly be perceived to be similar. From a purely practical point of view, however, similar means much the same as related.

Formal and Functional/Semantic Similarity

Cross-linguistic similarity is most obviously perceived on the basis of formally similar or identical individual items or words. The similarities may also be functional or semantic, in grammatical categories and semantic units, where no formal similarity is at hand. Grammatical similarities occur even across wholly unrelated languages. This was pointed out by Seppänen (1998), who listed seven grammatical correspondences between Finnish and English (basic word order, system of tenses, grammatical gender, possessive pronouns, marking of the genitive, the singular/plural contrast and the structure many/*moni* + noun). Several of these parallels occur also between Finnish and other Germanic languages. Seppänen's paper is written from a linguist's perspective, and we may assume that Finnish learners of English as well as English learners of Finnish would need proper guidance in order to make efficient use of these correspondences. Later in this book (pp. 79f. and Appendix 2), I show that structural similarities between Finnish and Swahili facilitated at least one learner's task.

In grammar, functional cross-linguistic similarity is what matters. How easily the learner can establish working one-to-one correspondences between grammatical elements largely depends on the degree of congruence, the similarity of the functions of grammatical categories (see below, pp. 68ff.). To establish such functional similarities, consciously or not, is essential, and an understanding of basic linguistic structures in the TL is a prerequisite for understanding and learning lexical items. Learners of closely related languages already have at least most of this basic understanding built in, while learners of wholly different languages have to put in considerable effort to acquire knowledge of what the different structures entail.

In lexis, formal similarity to an existing L1 word is perceived first, in that getting the word form precedes getting the word meaning. If formal similarity can be established, it provides the basis for a subsequent assumption of an associated translation equivalence (cf. Zimmermann, 1987). Formal correspondences arouse hopes of semantic or functional equivalence. Such hopes are often fulfilled in related languages, where formal cross-linguistic similarity normally goes together with some semantic similarity, though not always semantic identity. After meeting a word that is formally and semantically similar to the L1 word, the learner does not need to expend much effort on storing it in his mental lexicon. What is needed is merely a mental note 'this word in a similar form works in L2, too'. See further the section on cognates below.

Notes

1. Ard and Homburg's (1983) treatment of differences in test-taking results between Spanish and Arabic learners of English in the US is narrowly focused on the linguistic differences between Spanish- and Arabic-speaking university students, without consideration of the highly relevant factor of cultural and educational differences between the two groups. Their mapping of the lexical similarities between English and Spanish is, however, valuable.

Chapter 3

Learner Expectations, On-line Comprehension and Receptive Learning

In the next two chapters I will look at the concept of cross-linguistic similarity from several angles, trying to keep in the foreground what the learner does. As far as possible, I will attempt a chronological approach, beginning with the learner's expectations of what a new language to be learnt will be like. Basically, learners assume that the items (words) will be different, but that the system of the TL will work more or less in the same way as their L1 or some other language known to them.[1]

This set of expectations and beliefs concerns the phonemes, the grammatical structure and the pragmatics of the new language: these are assumed to exhibit cross-linguistic similarities until they have been found or shown to be different. Odlin (1989: 142) also makes this point: 'Research indicates that when everything else is equal, transfer will most likely result from a learner's judgment ... that particular structures in a previously learned language are quite like – if not the same as – structures in the target language' (cf. Swan, 1985: 85ff.).

Learning a TL perceived to be similar to the L1 means finding that target language texts have a number of items that at least roughly correspond in form and function/meaning to items in the L1. Simplified cross-linguistic one-to-one relationships can then be established between the items, contributing to at least an approximate understanding of text. In on-line comprehension, forms of items are recognised and comprehended first, while the functions of items are understood only later. Formal cross-linguistic similarities across related languages thus facilitate comprehension considerably. If, on the other hand, cross-linguistic similarities cannot be perceived, and considerable cultural differences are also at hand (as is the case when European learners are confronted with a language such as Chinese), the new learner has the more complex task of often having to establish a one-to-one relationship between a concept and a linguistic TL form. Cultural differences prevent cross-linguistic correspondences being naturally established between items.

Understanding an Unfamiliar Language

There have been a few studies of the role played by prior linguistic knowledge when learners encounter a text in a wholly unfamiliar language (e.g. Lorch & Meara, 1989). Singleton and Little (1984/2005) studied the degree to which native speakers of English were able to understand a text in Dutch. Some of the subjects knew German and these subjects made use of their German knowledge, performing much better than those who had French, but no German. In a similar study by Gibson and Hufeisen (2003), the subjects from a variety of L1s who knew English and/or German were, aided by a picture, to translate a text from Swedish. English and especially German were found to be useful first languages for understanding Swedish, whereas Hungarian, Portuguese and the Slavic languages were not.

These studies confirm the general common-sense view that learners, when trying to make sense of unfamiliar texts, look for facilitating cross-linguistic similarities wherever possible, and that a language related to the TL provides much more concrete help than an unrelated language. The studies mentioned focused on vocabulary, but parallels in grammar must also have played an important role for the subjects, in that the learner notices, probably subconsciously, that the structure of a related target language at least to some extent conforms to his expectations.

A related question is how much a child learner knows of a TL before actively starting to use it or study it at school. Such knowledge would be lexical and there have been some studies of this in Finland. Differences between Finnish-speaking and Swedish-speaking children in this respect indicate general differences between learners of a related and an unrelated target language. Palmberg (1985) showed that Swedish-speaking 10-year-olds in Finland knew a fair number of spoken English words before they began to read English at school. Forty concrete high-frequency words were tested, and all 74 children knew some of them. Fifteen out of the 20 that were most frequently understood showed close phonological and semantic similarity to the Swedish equivalent.[2]

A later, similar study by Pitkänen (1991) that focused on Finnish-speaking children, unsurprisingly enough, revealed a much smaller number of understood words. Pitkänen was unaware of Palmberg's work, but Rainio (2003) compared the two with an additional test of both Finnish and Swedish children. The mean solution percentages for the 14 words in common were 42% for the Finns and 68% for the Swedes.

If the TL is closely related to the L1, learners already have a considerable *potential vocabulary* in that language (see the section on cognates, pp. 73ff.).

Receptive mastery of a basic vocabulary in a closely related L2 can be achieved without much learning effort.

The Comprehension of Closely Related Languages: Scandinavia

If two languages are close enough, communication generally works when all people concerned speak their respective L1s. An area in Europe where such a problem-free international situation exists is Scandinavia. The Nordic countries, including not only Scandinavia proper (Sweden, Norway and Denmark), but also Finland and Iceland, have considerable cultural homogeneity, combined with a general feeling of affinity: the countries are felt to belong together for a great many historical and cultural reasons. 'Nordic unity' has been repeatedly stressed in various political and cultural contexts and still has a fairly firm grounding, even if EU membership has divided the five Nordic countries into two groups, with Norway and Iceland outside the EU, and Sweden, Denmark and Finland inside. The standard varieties of Swedish, Norwegian and Danish are similar enough for easy comprehension of written texts to be possible anywhere. Cross-linguistic formal and functional similarities to L1 are easily seen in all areas of another Scandinavian language. At least if the learner has had a little efficient teaching or guidance on the main differences in pronunciation and on some of the most common 'false friends' in vocabulary, oral communication also generally works well for speakers of standard varieties of the Scandinavian languages. The mutual comprehensibility of these languages means that it is not necessary to learn to produce something in another Scandinavian language: for communication to work it is sufficient to understand the other language, and you can also rely on your communication partner to understand you, when you speak your own language. Still, some variation exists and the problems of these communicative situations are not always symmetrical. Swedes were found to have more difficulties understanding Danish than Danes have understanding Swedish. Inter-Scandinavian communication is frequently discussed within Scandinavia (e.g. Elert, 1981; Maurud, 1976). A recent extensive survey (INS, 2004) investigated teenagers' Scandinavian language comprehension in all Nordic countries, including Finland, the Faeroes and Greenland. The preliminary results of the project provide new supplementary information, which reveals a few minor differences from the results of previous studies.[3] As for production in ordinary communicative situations, Scandinavians generally do not even attempt to sound native-like in a neighbouring language, since communication works anyway. Those who have crossed the border to live or stay in another country may try a little harder to sound native-like, at least on some occasions. But taking on a new linguistic identity and, connected with this, a new cultural identity if you are staying in a new country, is a sensitive matter. People range all the way from making eager attempts at perfection in the new language to a more usual, conscious objection to any modification of L1 patterns in an inter-Scandinavian context. Only if a Swede has exceptionally strong integrative motivation will he try to be truly Danish-like in his speech.

Finland occupies a special place in Nordic interchange. After minor initial problems, usually involving comprehension of spoken Danish, Finns who have Swedish as their L1 generally manage reasonably well in an inter-Scandinavian situation. For most Finnish speakers, however, this is not the case. Educated Finns usually have at least a basic knowledge from school of L2- or L3-Swedish, but in oral communication this is seldom sufficient for even moderate success in an inter-Scandinavian context. Unless Finns have spent time in Norway or Denmark, they have considerable problems when confronted with spoken Norwegian or (especially) spoken Danish. Their school Swedish may be sufficient for understanding the language of most speakers in Sweden, but their comprehension of spoken Danish is generally very limited at first. A Finn's situation in Denmark has been compared to an American who on the basis of his Spanish at school tries to understand spoken Portuguese (Lehtonen, 2002: 142). Since most Finnish speakers nowadays know more English than Swedish, they often prefer to communicate in English in inter-Nordic contexts. The contributions by Lehtonen and Tevajärvi in Elert (1981) deal with the problems that Finnish speakers meet with Scandinavian speakers. Such problems occur mainly in listening: communicative success in inter-Scandinavian oral contexts seems to require (near-)nativeness or at least fluency in one Scandinavian language. On the other hand, it is not overly difficult for Finns with a fair knowledge of school Swedish to learn to read Norwegian or Danish if they set their minds to it.

A project aimed at facilitating comprehension between Dutch and the Scandinavian languages was conducted in an Umeå University language teaching experiment, which sought to create a communicative situation between Dutchmen and Scandinavians similar to that existing within Scandinavia (Hedqvist, 1985; Strangert & Hedqvist, 1989). With some teaching concentrating on the main differences between Dutch on one hand and Danish or Swedish on the other, university students in both Holland and Scandinavia seemed to achieve a basic receptive competence in the other Germanic language in a relatively short time.

The comprehension of neighbouring Scandinavian languages provided part of the impetus for the EuroCom project (see below, pp. 103f.). An ambitious project utilising existing cross-linguistic similarities between related languages has thus been established, and work along these lines will no doubt continue to produce interesting and valuable material facilitating intercomprehension.

On-line Comprehension and Receptive Learning

Vocabulary is absolutely central where comprehension and receptive learning are concerned. The concept of cross-linguistic lexical similarity should be seen in a chronological perspective. We need to have an idea of the temporal relationships in vocabulary learning, what the stages are for learning new words. Hatch and Brown (1995: 372ff.), basing their model on Brown and Payne (1994), outline five essential steps in vocabulary learning: encountering a new word, getting the word form, getting the word meaning, consolidating word form and word meaning in memory, and using the word.

The first stage in vocabulary learning is recognising the word as a word when you encounter it. Here the advantage of having a formally similar word in your L1 repertoire is obvious; it is not necessary to perceive functional or semantic similarity at this stage. An English learner can read aloud sentences in another language that uses the Roman alphabet, without understanding its content. Where there is a zero similarity relation, as when learning a language with a wholly different writing system, even reaching this first stage takes some time. Learning Russian means that you first have to master the Russian alphabet and its rough correspondences to the sounds of your L1. The Arabic or Japanese script poses even greater problems.

Recognising the word, getting the word form and getting the meaning are part of the comprehension process, which is a prerequisite for learning. Learning, as distinct from comprehension, enters the picture when the focus is on the fourth stage in the process, consolidating word form and word meaning in memory.

The distinction between (on-line) comprehension and learning for comprehension is in theory quite clear, though the terminology varies. It is akin to the distinction between competence and performance and to a related, well-known point made by Corder (1967) and many others: the distinction between linguistic input and intake (mental registration of the input). The linguistic input undergoes two types of processing to become intake: Sharwood Smith (1986) distinguishes between processing for meaning and processing for competence change. Other pairs of terms used are vocabulary-inferring components and vocabulary-remembering components (Pressley *et al.*, 1987: 108), and discovering meaning and consolidating meaning (Schmitt, 1997). In these pairs only the latter type of processing can classify as learning. The terminology to be used here is on-line comprehension and receptive learning. Learning is not possible without some prior comprehension. But communication and learning processes interact, they 'operate ... at different levels of consciousness. If the wish to communicate is in focus ... there may be a process of learning taking place simultaneously' (Faerch *et al.*, 1984: 186). However, relating an item to prior knowledge (performance in comprehension) does not automatically involve a change in competence (receptive learning).

Comprehension relies on three types of information: *input* (linguistic and other communicative), *knowledge* (linguistic knowledge and world knowledge) and *context* (linguistic context and situational context). A key concept for on-line comprehension is inferencing. When meeting an unfamiliar word in a text, a learner can rely on different cues to work out its meaning: cross-linguistic, intra-lingual and contextual. What is also important is pragmatic knowledge, knowledge of the world. Contextual top-down cues interact with bottom-up cues that rely on the form of new words: at first the learner might make up an erroneous hypothesis about its meaning, but the context can serve as a corrective by helping the reader or listener to get back on the right track. In adult L1 comprehension the integration between top-down and bottom-up procedures is efficient. Advanced learners, too, are relatively successful in managing this, while learners at earlier stages tend to rely too much on either top-down or bottom-up procedures, whilst lacking the ability to integrate them (Haastrup, 1991: 342; see also Vaurio, 1998). For L2 comprehension, a learner often has to rely on context and extra-linguistic background, top-down knowledge, to fill in for deficiencies in word recognition. In order to be able to read fluently learners need to have good mastery of a sufficient number of high-frequency words. They can then recognise the orthographical forms of words in an automatic and relatively error-free way (Schmitt & McCarthy, 1997: 4), thus freeing their mental capacity for higher levels of comprehension.

In on-line comprehension, forms of items are recognised first. The comprehension of functions or meanings of items comes later – though previous relevant grammatical knowledge, usually L1 knowledge, serves as an underlying basis facilitating comprehension. Before new words and structures can be learned, the learner must first comprehend them. Comprehension of a word normally means that a new TL item can be matched with an existing L1 item. Especially if the items are formally similar, this procedure is much more concrete than connecting a new item with a concept.[4] Occasionally the learner may, of course, make erroneous assumptions about the exact meaning of a new item, and to avoid this the learner must check the linguistic similarities against top-down processes. Only part of what is comprehended at one time is actually learned, but at a later stage, comprehension (mostly only repeated comprehension) develops into receptive learning. This means that there has been a change in memory so that an approximate L1-equivalent can be retrieved from an L2-stimulus.

One aspect of the distinction between comprehension and learning is the different significance of contextual cues. In on-line comprehension, contextual as well as extra-linguistic cues (knowledge of the world) are essential. Learners do not need to understand every single word in a text they read, they can attain comprehension, at least approximate comprehension, on the strength of the surrounding linguistic and situational context and/or extra-linguistic knowledge. For receptive learning, on the other hand, contextual cues do not have the same significance. In the words of Pressley *et al.* (1987: 108) 'learners can derive vocabulary meanings from context, but this process alone does not foster retention of meaning'. Contextual cues have a definite role in on-line comprehension, and they are not directly connected with linguistic similarity. But in order to anchor the word in the mental lexicon, to *learn* the word, the learner will be mainly helped by linguistic cues, either cross-linguistic or intralinguistic (see Haastrup, 1991, who distinguishes between the guessability and the learnability of a word; Mondria & Wit-deBoer, 1991). How easily a word can be matched with an already-existing L1 word largely determines the relative ease or difficulty of comprehension. Formal similarities, cross-linguistic or intralinguistic, clearly facilitate such matching: they provide many opportunities for easy effortless comprehension, which in its turn also makes learning easier. As learning progresses, the learner's mistaken or oversimplified hypotheses can be rectified.

Thus, while on-line comprehension is often facilitated by contextual and extralinguistic cues, receptive learning at the beginning above all relies on how easily the new word can be linked in the mental lexicon to existing formally and/or semantically similar items. Storing new items in memory will operate largely on the basis of cross-linguistic and intralinguistic similarities: how naturally relations can be established to items already known. It is natural for a learner to assume that if a word in another language is formally similar to an L1 word, it will also have an identical, or at least a similar, meaning. Lotto and de Groot (1998: 59 f.), referring to Kirsner *et al.* (1993), make the point that 'learning cognates does not involve creating a new entry in memory, but rather adding new information to an existing entry.'

The preliminary stage of on-line comprehension is tied to the concept of language *intelligibility*, which apparently depends at least as much on grammatical as on lexical similarity. Nation (1990: 37) points out that if a word occurs in grammatical patterns which are similar to the patterns in which its translation occurs in the L1, this part of the learning burden will be light. Similarity of grammar appears to be especially important in facilitating *learning* (cf. Ellegård, 1978: 195), both learning for comprehension and learning for production. Lexical similarity, which facilitates the learner's linking words to other, formally similar words, is also basic for learning, but it may not work in exactly the same way for comprehension, as comprehension can be merely approximate and comprehension in itself does not leave a permanent mark in the mental lexicon. Cross-linguistic similarity facilitates both on-line comprehension and receptive learning, but in slightly different ways. A word that is easily guessable may not be as easily learnable.

Notes

1. Knowledge of other languages than the L1 is, of course, also highly relevant, but to avoid clumsiness, L1 is the term used in this chapter, and often elsewhere in the book, for 'L1 or some other language known to the learner'. See the section on non-native transfer, pp. 78ff.
2. These 15 words, with their Swedish equivalents, were the following: sister – *syster* (solution percentage 100%), hand – *hand* (95%), cat – *katt* (89%), school – *skola* (82%), father – *fa(de)r* (82%), mother – *mo(de)r* (81%), policeman – *polis* (81%), blue – *blå* (81%), house – *hus* (77%), dance – *dans* (77%), room – *rum* (69%), drink – *dricka, drink, dryck* (66%), brother – *bro(de)r* (65), snow – *snö* (53%) and foot – *fot* (50%) (Palmberg 1985). The five words in Palmberg's list which he defines as phonologically different from their Swedish equivalents, but which also scored high, were dog – *hund* (85%), love – *kärlek* (80%), boy – *pojke* (80%), girl – *flicka* (77%) and name – *namn* (57%). When the children were asked to state where they thought they had learnt the English words, the five most popular responses were (1) watching TV, (2) listening to music, (3) at home (in general), (4) from friends and (5) travelling.
3. The INS project, based in Lund, presents a comprehensive picture of how well teenagers (aged 16–19 at the upper secondary level) in the Nordic countries cope with understanding neigbouring languages today. The figures are also compared with results in a test of English listening comprehension. As in Maurud's (1976) study, the Norwegians had the best results. This is probably partly due to Norwegians being used to hearing an exceptionally wide variety of Norwegian dialects. There are even two varieties of standard Norwegian: Bokmål, mainly the language of the capital, and Nynorsk, a compilation based on West coast dialects, artificially constructed in the 19th century. Swedes, Danes and Swedish-speaking Finns were roughly equal, while Finns, as expected, had much lower figures. The subjects in the capitals, Stockholm and Copenhagen, did much less well than the ones in Malmö and Århus. In the English

comprehension test, the Finns did fairly well and, in fact, had slightly better results than the Danes, though they did not reach the standard of the Swedish Finns, the Faeroe Islanders, the Icelanders, the Norwegians and the Swedes, who were placed in that order. One interesting fact is that the teenagers' parents, who were also tested in comprehension of neighbouring languages, had consistently better results than their children.

4. Compare what happens in attrition. With increasing age, we tend to forget names of people and objects very easily. It seems that such labels are not very closely linked to other lexical items in the network, and they can therefore easily disappear, at least momentarily. Close links with other lexical items apparently provide helpful stimuli to recovery of the form searched for.

Chapter 4

Cross-linguistic Similarities in Comprehension and Production: The Mental Lexicon

L1 Comprehension and L1 Production

L1 research has focused more than SLA research has on the relationship between comprehension and production (see, for example, Clark, 1993; Clark & Hecht, 1983; D. Ingram, 1974). There are certainly differences between L1 acquisition and SLA, mainly due to the difference in maturity between children and adult second language learners, and to fact that the learners have already acquired at least one language. Yet the main characteristics of the processes underlying L2 comprehension and L2 production can hardly be all that different from the equivalent processes in L1. At least established relations between L1 comprehension and L1 production are no doubt highly relevant also for the relation between L2 comprehension and L2 production. Both children and learners try to perceive similarities to prior knowledge, and the fact that there are differences between the two kinds of prior knowledge must be of secondary importance. Advanced FL (foreign language) learners learn new words very much in the same way as native speakers (adolescents and adults) learn new words in their L1 (Meara, 1988: 13).

I will now take up some of the salient points made by researchers about the relation between L1 comprehension and L1 production. The study of speech errors throws light on the ways in which formal and semantic similarity works on L1 communication. Fay and Cutler (1977) analyse malapropisms and list other types of speech errors: spoonerisms, anticipations, perseverations, omissions and blends – see also, for example, Aitchison (1976: 208ff.) and Heikkinen and Valo (1984) on slips in interaction, and Laufer (1988) on synforms. The underlying reason for one type of speech error is formal similarity between words. In a true malapropism, no semantic similarity is present. A well-known example is Mrs Malaprop's saying 'She's as headstrong as an allegory on the banks of the Nile'. Another malapropism is 'You keep new-born chicks warm in an incinerator' (for incubator). Further examples of malapropisms are *emancipated* for intended *emaciated, insect* for *index,* and *experience* for *experiment.* Such activation of a formally-similar word occurs in the production mechanism, but intra-lingual formal similarity leading to misinterpretation of words may also affect comprehension, though this aspect does not appear to have been much studied.

There are other types of native speakers' speech error apart from malapropisms caused by similarity of form. Slips of the tongue are most often caused by semantic similarity, without formal similarity being involved. It is quite common for native speakers to make a selection error and produce an antonym (*good* for *bad, summer* for *winter, midsummer* for *New Year*) or a hyponym or another word with a clear semantic relation to the intended one (*fingers* for *toes*). However, such errors, which the speaker himself often immediately notices, do not occur in L1 comprehension. If somebody utters the word *summer* we interpret it as referring to that season, unless the context leads us to suspect irony or that there has been a speech error. In simple terms a speech error can be described like this: the intended word and a semantically or phonologically similar word are stored close enough for them both to be activated in the production process, and the wrong selection is made. An error in reception may occur owing to confusion of phonologically-similar words, but because they are helped by the surrounding context native speakers are normally able to avoid confusing semantically-similar words in the comprehension process.

In both comprehension and production, form and meaning are paired, but different retrieval procedures are used, and the relationship is not symmetrical. The absence of semantically-based slips in L1 comprehension pinpoints the difference between the two processes of comprehension and production. A word that is formally or semantically similar to the intended one can be easily activated in production, but in comprehension semantically-related words dissimilar in form from the intended one are not activated to the extent that they would compete with the word in the input. Generally speaking, formal similarity, but not semantic similarity, may cause confusion in L1 comprehension.

Both comprehension and production need to be considered for a thorough understanding of the underlying processes of language learning. Clark summarises her discussion of the problem in the following way:

> To conclude, there must be different representations for comprehension and production, so both processes can be taken into account in any theory of acquisition. Accounts based on production alone, or comprehension alone, are necessarily incomplete. This view is incompatible with all accounts that simply take for granted that there is a single set of repre-

sentations in memory, neutral between comprehension and production, that captures the idealised speaker's linguistic knowledge. This overly simple view ignores both the asymmetry between comprehension and production observable in all speakers, regardless of age. And also the essential differences, for example, between the auditory information in C-representations and the articulatory information in P-representations. In acquisition, the asymmetry between the two types of representation plays a critical role in the alignment process. C-representations, set up first, offer a means of checking and, where necessary, adjusting the products of early P-representations. (Clark, 1993: 251)

L2 Comprehension and L2 Production

Compared with what has been done in L1-acquisition research, SLA research is narrower in scope. In general, L1-research has been conducted along three different lines: language comprehension, language production and language development. Of these, language production has been the most extensively studied area in SLA research, so much so that learning for production, especially learning grammar, has often at least implicitly been identified with SLA generally. The implications of the work up to the late 1980s, even that of a key figure such as Corder, whose contributions to SLA theory have been of major importance, are that language comprehension and vocabulary studies are, as it were, stepchildren not worthy of treatment at the same level as the study of grammar acquisition for productive use.

Essential in an SLA context is the temporal precedence of comprehension over learning and production. Before items or structures of a new language can be produced, the learner first has to comprehend them. Some comprehension has to occur before production, though it need not be complete prior to production (Clark & Hecht, 1983).[1]

What has often been done in SLA research is to talk about learning problems when the matter under discussion is actually problems in the production mechanisms. The interaction between comprehension and production is also more complex in SLA than in L1-acquisition, where it is easier to get a full picture of the learner's output at various stages. If a consistent distinction is made between learning for comprehension and learning for production this question may be elucidated. Ability to produce presupposes some previous understanding of the underlying systems of phonology, grammar and lexis, while ability to comprehend does so to a much more limited extent, for at least approximate comprehension to occur. If a learner's expectations of general structural similarity between L1 and the TL are at least in essential parts fulfilled, learning for comprehension can concentrate on salient lexical items, nouns, adjectives and verbs, after a few hundred high-frequency words, including function words, have been mastered. Comprehension focuses on decoding of contextual meaning while structural details remain in the background. Grammaticality and acceptability are concepts far less important to the listener or reader than to the speaker or writer. For English learners, learning the German genders is a main obstacle in L2 production, but it affects L2 comprehension only in a limited way. Fay and Cutler (1977) as well as Channell (1988) discuss the different directional relations between form (sound) and meaning in comprehension and production.

> The two distinct processes of production ... and comprehension make differential use of the store of words in the mind. Part of the production process must consist of the selection of appropriate words according to the meaning to be conveyed. The word form is then converted into a phonological shape for onward processing into speech. Thus the direction is meaning to sound. In comprehension, the direction of mapping is sound to meaning. These differences might suggest that for the mental word store the optimal arrangement for comprehension will be according to sound. (Channell, 1988: 85)

Comprehension and production are modes of use relying on different retrieval procedures, and for easy retrieval procedures in L2 comprehension it is essential how much similarity to prior knowledge, formal and functional, has been perceived. For L2 comprehension, the importance of form is manifested in the learners' making use of both intra-lingual similarities and cross-linguistic similarities. For production, again, simple cross-linguistic similarities of form are not as naturally exploited, since the learner starts out from a vague communicative intention, to which various phonological and syntactic procedures are applied.

While good learners may acquire a considerable receptive proficiency, at least of a psychotypologically close language, in a surprisingly short time, achieving advanced speaking or writing ability is much more complex and time-consuming. The different speeds of learning are also connected with the difference between declarative knowledge, ('knowledge that') and procedural knowledge ('knowledge how'). In philosophy, the distinction between declarative and procedural knowledge was made by Ryle (1949). Faerch and Kasper (1987), among others, have used the distinction in SLA research. In reading comprehension, declarative knowledge of vocabulary can take the learner a long way. It may develop rapidly and suddenly, whereas the development of procedural knowledge requires a great deal of time and practice. The relation between declarative and procedural knowledge is further discussed by deKeyser (2005), and earlier by, among others, J.R. Anderson (1983), Anderson & Lebriere (1988) and Singley & Anderson (1989). See also below, p. 91.

The presence or absence of perceived cross-linguistic similarity in comprehension is highly relevant for the varying gap existing between learners' receptive and productive vocabulary. That native speakers can understand many more words than they can produce is self-evident. The same asymmetry is generally true of L2 learners, at least if they have had an extensive L2-input, having learnt the language in a natural environment. There are, however, variations here, in that some learning situations can be found where the gap is very small, almost non-existent. This was the result of Takala's 1984 study, which investigated young Finnish learners of English in a predominantly rural classroom environment in the 1970s, a time when such learners had hardly any L2 input outside the classroom. The near-zero similarity relation between Finnish and English, combined with the limited L2 input, explains the insignificant difference between the receptive and productive vocabularies of these learners. The learning situation of the classroom is quite different from learning in a natural context where there is a wealth of unstructured linguistic input. Similar to the Finnish situation, English speakers learning, say, Arabic or Chinese entirely in a normal classroom context will not be able to understand much more than they can produce. It is almost impossible to tell whether the limited input of a classroom learning situation or the scarcity of perceived similarities for comprehension is the more powerful factor in reducing the normal gap between comprehension and production, but both are clearly important.[2] Another factor in the classroom situation that may contribute to reducing the gap between receptive and productive control of vocabulary is that teachers may require students to produce words whose meanings are not altogether clear to them (see Channell, 1988: 84f.).

There are, then, basic differences between L2-comprehension and L2-production that need to be spelled out, also because cross-linguistic similarity works differently on the two. Lado (1957: 59) commented on the existence of such differences some time ago. A general difference concerns the approximate nature of all comprehension. Although comprehension is often approximate, communication, aided by linguistic and situational context, may still work: one need not understand every detail and every shade of meaning of a message to comprehend its general content.[3] Even native speakers are far from perfect in interpreting a communication partner's intentions.

Learners have choice problems in both comprehension and production: they have to choose between competing activated items. But in production the learner is faced with a number of choices, not only between different words, but also between different forms of the same word. Above all, the speaker/writer has to activate the knowledge structures himself, without external stimuli.

In comprehension the learner establishes relationships between incoming data and existing knowledge structures in the mind. Comprehension takes place when input and knowledge match each other. The form of a word is already given and it is mapped on to relevant existing knowledge, while in production the speaker himself has to give linguistic form to a preverbal intention. When you decide to say something, you 'create a meaning and then search for the word form associated with just that meaning' (Clark, 1993: 249). In production, the function that has to be given linguistic form must originate in the learner's mind. Comprehension and production 'use linguistic rules for different purposes and hence require different processing' (Garnham, 1985: 221). Production requires definite sentence plans for the messages. This means that a greater task effort is required by the learner in production than in comprehension (see Paradis, 1985: 27f.). Production does not have a clearly defined external situational context. It places much greater demands on specificity and accuracy than comprehension does. Similarities between incoming data and existing knowledge structures are more concrete and tangible than similarities between communicative intentions and assumed existing knowledge structures, and here lies an important reason why formal cross-linguistic similarities play a more important part in L2-comprehension than in L2-production. Cross-linguistically similar words, which form the central part of the learner's potential vocabulary, facilitate the learner's task in comprehension, but not at all to the same extent in production. The learner will not use L2 items productively until they, or parts of them, have been learned, but the potential knowledge across languages perceived to be similar is used for comprehension before learning has taken place. Mackey's early work already mentions the facilitative effect of L1 transfer on comprehension (1965: 109f.). Existing knowledge structures are activated by incoming data, all the more so if cross-linguistic or other formal similarities can be established, as they can in comprehension of closely related languages.

Perceived and Assumed Similarity

This leads on to a formulation of another basic difference between comprehension and production of foreign languages. Here the sequence in which the processes are taking place must be considered. In comprehension of related languages, learners can often start out by *perceiving* cross-linguistic similarity (i.e. formal similarity), to elements of a language they already know. A subsequent stage is the *assumption* of an associated semantic and/or functional similarity. If no formal similarity can be perceived, the learner will have to make do with merely assuming that the languages work in much the same way. Thus, in production and in comprehension of totally distant languages, assumptions provide the starting point: learners merely assume that a similarity exists to a language whose details they do not know (see Jarvis, 1997: 328: 'the source for L1 influence is always an assumed similarity between the L1 and the L2'). Assumption can be and often is based on previous perception, but that is not always the case. For two of the three similarity relations outlined above (similarity, difference and zero relations), perceived and assumed similarity are difficult to distinguish from each other, partly because comprehension and production normally work in constant interaction.[4] This is most obvious across related languages. When there is a zero similarity relation, however, there is a difference between comprehension and production in the extent of transfer, positive transfer. In target languages very distant from the L1, there will normally be little or no visible transfer in comprehension and learning, but transfer will occur in production, when the learner does not perceive but merely assumes that items and systems in the target language will work in more or less the same way as in L1 or some other known language. L1-procedures are used because relevant L2-procedures are not available, and the result is often a large number of errors, many of which may affect the comprehensibility of the message.

The difference between perceived and assumed similarity recalls the discussion of transfer to somewhere/ transfer to nowhere (Andersen, 1983; Kellerman, 1995; see also Jarvis, 1997; Odlin, 2003). Andersen restricts his discussion to syntactic transfer. He says that one of the two conditions for transfer to appear is that the learner must perceive similarity between an element in the L2 and a corresponding element in L1: there must be transfer to somewhere.

Kellerman states that, if cross-linguistic similarity is the driving force behind transfer, then where there is no perceived similarity, there should be no transfer. I do not quite see that this would directly follow from Andersen's argument. Anyway, Kellerman (1995: 137) proposes a refinement of this principle to complement Andersen: that there can be transfer 'which is not licensed by similarity to the L2'. Now, it seems possible to consider Kellerman's examples as instances where Andersen's principle does, in fact, apply (Odlin, 2003: 456). The difference between transfer to somewhere and transfer to nowhere appears to be another way of phrasing the difference between perceived similarity and assumed similarity, and it also relates to the differences between similarity, contrast and lack of similarity, discussed above. With Andersen and Jarvis, we can certainly agree that similarity is the driving force behind transfer. Likewise, there is no reason to doubt Kellerman's view that transfer can occur where no perceived similarity is involved. Schachter (1983: 104) also makes the point that 'one's L1 knowledge has as much influence on the learning of an unrelated second language as on the learning of a related one', it just takes different forms. Transfer to somewhere is predominantly positive, and is particularly clearly manifested in comprehension and across languages perceived to be similar, whereas transfer to nowhere mostly corresponds to negative transfer or interference in learner production and across distant languages.

The somewhere/nowhere debate illustrates the possibility of looking at transfer from two points of view, both of them perfectly justifiable. The differences can be explained by researchers focusing on different types and aspects of transfer. An attempt to rephrase the issues placing them in a wider context, including communication and learning, comprehension and production could be something like the following:

> Transfer as a communication process is the use of perceived and assumed cross-linguistic similarities in L2 comprehension and L2 production. It is natural to perceive similarities across closely-related languages, and they are especially frequently employed in comprehension. Formal similarity of items as well as functional equivalence of categories are relevant for the extent of perceived similarities in comprehension. Where similarities cannot be perceived, as in production and in comprehension of very distant languages, they are merely assumed. The learner assumes that L1 forms and L1 procedures are relevant and helpful for L2 production but, when similarities are merely assumed, without prior perception, there is a considerable risk of errors.

> Transfer, or cross-linguistic influence, as a learning process is what transfer as a communication process may result in: it means that L1 items and L1 procedures have become or are becoming part of the learner's interlanguage system.

Cross-linguistic Similarity and the Mental Lexicon

The question how the mental lexicon of a bi- or multilingual is organised has been discussed in a variety of contexts (for some recent contributions, see, for example, Cenoz *et al.*, 2003; De Bot, 2004; Kroll & Dijkstra, 2002; Singleton, 1999). Not all that much has been said about the relevance of cross-linguistic similarity to the representation of words in the mind, but what Paradis (1987: 16) said almost 20 years ago no doubt still holds true: 'The less two languages have in common, the more they are represented separately'.

Word association tests provide evidence of what type of words are most closely linked with each other in the mind. In these tests a subject is asked to say the first word that comes to mind when presented with a stimulus. Tests with native speakers have shown considerable stereotypy: adults reacting in fairly predictable ways to the stimulus words, with little variation (Postman & Keppel, 1970). There are basically two types of responses, syntagmatic (*door* as a response to *shut*) and paradigmatic (*chair* as a response to *table*), the latter being generally more frequent than the former. Young children seem to prefer syntagmatic responses, and they differ from adults above all in that they also produce a fairly large number of 'clang associates' (*but* as a response to *butter*) (e.g. Ervin, 1961). These are words phonetically similar but without a semantic or syntactic relation to the stimulus word. Native speakers thus appear to show some development in the organisation of their mental lexicon: as maturity and L1 proficiency increase, words appear to be organised in the lexicon more and more by content, not by form. Several other researchers have arrived at the same conclusion.

Word association tests have also been used with foreign language learners (Meara, 1978, 1982; Schmitt & Meara, 1997; Söderman, 1993; cf. Singleton & Little, 1991) to clarify whether there might be differences between native speakers and learners in the organisation of their mental lexicon. Non-native subjects do not respond to L1 stimuli in quite the same way as native speakers, but they show similarities to native children. They are often influenced by the phonological or orthographic form of the stimulus word ('clang responses') and they also show more variation from subject to subject in their responses. Söderman's study analysed Swedish-speaking subjects in Finland at four different proficiency levels and found that there was a steady development from clang and other unusual responses to syntagmatic and especially paradigmatic responses. Responses by the highest proficiency level (university students of English) in Söderman's subjects show that the distributional pattern still does not quite reach native speaker level, but 'the more proficient a learner gets, the stronger the words are integrated in his lexicon and the fewer unusual responses will he produce' (Söderman,1993: 149). Non-native development thus parallels native development in that the organisation of the mental lexicon on the basis of phonological similarity is gradually being replaced by a more semantically based organisation. However, Söderman also makes the point that the frequency level of the stimulus words plays an important part in the test. With high-frequency words there was hardly any difference between native speakers and advanced learners, while learners produced significantly more unusual responses, mostly based on purely formal similarity, than native speakers when the stimulus words were infrequent. Word frequency is thus a highly relevant variable closely interlinked with the learner's proficiency level. Lowie and Verspoor found for Dutch learners that:

> the degree to which L2 prepositions are similar to prepositions in L1 only affected the scores if these prepositions were not very frequent: for the frequently occurring prepositions no effect of similarity (i.e. transfer, HR) was found. The explanation for this finding would be that subjects tend to rely on their first language only for the more unfamiliar prepositions ... This interaction did not occur at the highest proficiency levels: these students had been sufficiently exposed to the L2 to develop full representations for all prepositions. (Lowie & Verspoor, 2004: 89)

Another area of research that reveals differences between native speakers and advanced learners is studies of reaction time in grammaticality judgments (e.g. Alanen, 1997).

Formal similarities, phonological and orthographical, have an essential role in the organisation of the mental lexicon, especially at early stages of learning. These similarities may be predominantly cross-linguistic or predominantly intralinguistic, with the proportion being determined largely by the distance perceived between L1 and L2 and by the proficiency of the learner. As learning progresses, the learner relies less on phonological similarity and more and more on semantic similarity, with advanced learners approaching but not quite reaching the native speaker's setup, which is primarily semantically organised. A few conclusions can be quoted from the many studies providing support for the development from form to meaning in the learner's mental lexicon: 'Formal processing does come prominently into play during the early acquisition of a given L2 lexical item, but such processing predominates only where semantic processes find no avenue for the making of semantic connections' (Singleton, 1994: 54). 'Lexical units are increasingly progressed *qua* meaning rather than *qua* form as their integration into the mental lexicon progresses' (Singleton, 1999: 189). 'Increasing fluency in the second language is associated with a reduction in reliance on form and an increase in reliance on meaning' (Kroll & de Groot, 1997: 174). See further, for example, Albert and Obler (1978: 57); Henning (1973); Joannopoulou (2002: 40); Meara (1978).

Notes

1. On the basis of a similar word formation occurring in L1, a Danish learner correctly produced the German compound *neusprachlich* without ever having come across it before (Faerch & Kasper, 1987: 128ff.). However, this cannot be taken as evidence for production preceding comprehension, since both elements of the compound must have been in the learner's L2 repertoire from before. Cf. what D. Ingram (1974: 316 says about grammar, 'Some comprehension of a specific grammatical form or construction occurs before it is produced.' Eckman (1981) makes the point that this may not always be the case in phonology, but the relation between the motor-perceptual skills of sound recognition and sound production may be different from the overall skills of language comprehension and production.

2. The relation between receptive and productive aspects of foreign language vocabulary has been discussed by Melka (1997) (see also Meara, 1990, 1997). Asymmetry between comprehension and production not only appears in lexis, it has also been found in phonology, as an early study by Nemser (1971) showed.

3. Flynn (1986: 135): 'Production tests principally evaluate a learner's developing structural competence in the L2. On the other hand, comprehension tests provide a less direct measure of structural competence and are significantly influenced by pragmatic context.'

4. Some studies have found that there is more interdependence, mutual dependence between L1 and L2 in comprehension than in production (Bergh 1986; Kolers, 1966). The consequence of this is that there is more transfer, more use of cross-linguistic similarities in L2 comprehension than in L2 production.

Chapter 5

Transfer: The Use of Cross-linguistic Similarities. The Finnish Scene

Transfer Studies: History and Limitations

From the 1960s to the 1980s, the term transfer, originally derived from behaviourist psychology, came in for a great deal of criticism for its unwanted associations. A better term might be cross-linguistic influence (see the introduction in Kellerman & Sharwood Smith, 1986), but since the word transfer still is the most commonly used term, and today appears to have lost at least most of its associations to structuralism and behaviourism, it is the term I will use in this book. Transfer is here used in a wide sense, corresponding to cross-linguistic influence. It thus covers the many different ways in which one language may influence (the learning of) another. For definitions and discussions of the term transfer, see Dechert and Raupach (1989: xiff.), Kellerman and Sharwood Smith (1986: 1ff.) and Odlin (1989: 28).

Positive vs. negative transfer

While it is comparatively easy to link certain types of errors to the L1, there are great problems in ascertaining to what extent the L1 has influenced good and correct expressions in learner language. The emphasis in transfer studies has thus consistently been on negative transfer, while positive transfer has at most been given some remarks in passing. The use of the evaluative adjectives positive and negative has been criticised by researchers primarily concerned with the processes underlying transfer (Faerch & Kasper, 1987; Sajavaara & Lehtonen, 1989). They are right in arguing that the distinction between positive and negative is relevant at the product level only, not the process level. Still, the question to what extent prior linguistic knowledge has a facilitative or inhibiting effect on learning is certainly important to anyone working in the field of second language acquisition. In fact, we need to distinguish not only between process and product, but also between two separate levels of processing, where one level precedes the other. What has been called interference or negative L1 transfer in L2 production could be better described as *absence of relevant concrete (positive) transfer, leading to subsequent wrong assumptions about cross-linguistic similarities between L1 and L2.* Positive transfer could then be described as 'the application of at least partially correct perceptions or assumptions of cross-linguistic similarity.' That perceptions only partially correct still have a mainly positive effect is particularly relevant for comprehension. But we need to broaden our approach to transfer. The many variables affecting transfer and their interaction need to be clarified first, and their possible negative or positive effects discussed separately. Such a full-scale study is hardly possible, at least not in the near future.

Ignorance is a term that has been used in connection with transfer. When ignorance has been discussed, it has usually been restricted to the context of language production, not comprehension. Ignorance lies behind production of many items and constructions in a totally unrelated language exhibiting a zero similarity relation to the L1. Then the resulting choice of words and constructions shows that the learner's assumptions about the L2 are unfounded. In such a situation the state of ignorance may have provoked 'a desperate casting about for lexical straws to clutch at' (Singleton & Little, 1991: 63). But for comprehension and for the production of psycho-typologically close languages, where there is constant interaction between perceived and assumed cross-linguistic similarities, the concept of ignorance is hardly helpful. It is a truism that if a learner produces an unacceptable word or construction of any kind, some degree of ignorance lies behind it.

It is noteworthy that researchers who neglected or played down the role of transfer in SLA, tended to restrict their discussion and examples to syntactic errors in learner production. This is much too narrow an approach. Generalisations about language transfer cannot be made on the exclusive basis of produced syntactic errors. As for example Jarvis (1997: 87) says, a broader methodological perspective than focusing on errors in production is clearly called for. Comprehension as well as vocabulary and other areas of language than syntax definitely need to be considered for a more complete picture of how the L1 influences the language learning process. As I see it, another related shortcoming in the attempts by Krashen (1985) and other researchers in the 1980s to underestimate transfer at least partly depends on preoccupation with syntax. There is also an implied idea that the nature of cross-linguistic influence is entirely negative. Yet there is overwhelming evidence that it is predominantly positive, though not exclusively so.

The insufficiency of transfer studies

From the process point of view, most transfer studies so far can be regarded as insufficient because they have focused on how only one type of similarity is made use of in production. Transfer studies have been concerned mainly with how assumed functional cross-linguistic similarities are manifested in production as errors, especially grammatical errors. Error analysis is, however, insufficient and its insufficiency (its focus being on what learners cannot do rather than on what they can do) was noted almost immediately after its introduction as a special branch of applied linguistics (see, for example, Hammarberg, 1974). Grammatical errors in production may well be the most amenable for analysis, but concentrating on them gives a one-sided picture of what type of cross-linguistic similarities there are, and how they actually are manifested. The question of what is actually transferred also needs to be clarified. Is it linguistic units, rules (or principles) and/or strategies? We certainly need to know more about this, and also about the questions how?, when? and why? relating to transfer.

These critical remarks do not mean that transfer studies so far have been worthless. On the contrary, a large number of valuable studies were made many decades ago, often as a side product of contrastive analysis (CA). As early as the 1950s, the books by Weinreich (1953) and Lado (1957) contained many perceptive observations. Lado's work in particular has, however, been unfairly treated by later linguists. A few isolated, somewhat unhappily phrased, oversimplifications in Lado's book have been frequently quoted and criticised, while little concrete attention has been paid to the many original ideas that later provided at least the indirect stimulus for CA as well as further work in SLA. Lado had a much more comprehensive approach to SLA than most later linguists.[1] He was concerned not only with grammar, but also with lexical, phonological and cultural aspects. He also made it clear that a list of learner problems arising from an undertaken contrastive analysis must be regarded as hypothetical until checked against the actual output of the learner. However, it was not until later, in the 1970s, that systematic error analysis came into the picture.[2] Most error analyses from that time were content to distinguish between two underlying reasons for errors, overgeneralisation of an L2 rule and L1 transfer. These two may, however, be regarded as two different linguistic manifestations of one psychological process – reliance on prior knowledge.

Early studies of transfer were closely linked to contrastive analysis (CA). The underlying idea of CA was the applied linguistic idea that comparative descriptions could form a basis for facilitating language learning and language teaching. Large-scale systematic contrastive analyses were undertaken for that purpose in the 1960s, both in Europe and the US. In the US, Stockwell *et al.* (1965) described a sophisticated attempt to establish hierarchies of difficulty on the basis of structural and functional–semantic correspondences. However, the American interest in contrastive analysis soon ebbed out, partly because the world of linguistic concepts is not readily compatible with concepts from the psychology of learning. In Europe, CA has enjoyed a longer life and has had a mainly theoretical slant. National projects were set up where aspects of English were compared with, for example, Polish, Hungarian, Serbo-Croat, Finnish and Swedish. The Polish project in particular has produced, and is still producing, a great many studies, primarily oriented towards theoretical linguistics, not applied linguistics. Early works on contrastive phonology are Nemser (1971), based on his 1961 dissertation, and Briére (1966). Selinker's studies (1966, 1969) are pioneer works in transfer which also treat syntactic transfer experimentally. Around 1970, however, a reaction set in, and the 1970s was a time when the role of the L1 in SLA was minimised, particularly in the US (Dulay & Burt, 1974; Dulay *et al.*, 1982; Krashen, 1985). Then, in 1977, came Kellerman's important paper and in the 1980s the negative attitude to transfer gradually changed. Anthologies and other books on transfer appeared (Dechert & Raupach, 1989; Gass & Selinker, 1983; Kellerman & Sharwood Smith, 1986; Ringbom, 1987; and above all Odlin, 1989). Among later discussions of transfer, Cenoz *et al.*(2001); R. Ellis (1995: Ch. 8); Gass (1996); Jarvis (1997, 2000); Jarvis and Odlin (2000); Kellerman (1995); Odlin (2003); Odlin and Jarvis (2004); and Selinker (1992: Ch. 7) may be specially mentioned.[3]

Today few linguists question the importance of language transfer (though some object to the use of the term transfer because of its supposed unwanted associations), but the detailed ways in which transfer works together with other variables are complex and anything approaching a full study remains to be carried out.

In their recent paper, Odlin and Jarvis (2004) mention the three factors of psychotypology, proficiency and overgeneralisation as being especially relevant to transfer studies, and stress the importance for future research of studying their interaction.

How should transfer be studied? One fruitful approach is to compare groups of learners of similar cultural and educational backgrounds but with different L1s learning the same foreign language. If the groups are not roughly equivalent from a cultural and educational point of view, no certain conclusions can be drawn about the linguistic factor causing possible differences.

The Language Scene in Finland: Characteristics of Finnish and Swedish

Finnish, Swedish and English in Finland

Finland is a country that is in many respects ideally suited for studies of second or third language acquisition. The two official languages of the country, Finnish and Swedish, are linguistically totally different. Culturally and educationally, however, the two language groups are as close as can be found in any country anywhere in the world. Finnish is spoken as L1 by more than 93% of the population and Swedish by about 6%, concentrated to the coastal areas in the south and west. Many if not most of the main towns are also located in these bilingual areas, but in the rest of the country Swedish is not heard at all, except for a few programmes on TV, where the language of the great majority of non-Finnish programmes anyway is English, normally with subtitles given in Finnish.

Some basic facts of Finnish history are necessary to understand the language situation. Without knowledge of the historical background it is difficult for a foreigner to understand, for example, the special official language status accorded to Swedish, although today most Finns speak better English than Swedish. (For a fuller account of the language situation in Finland, see, for example, Ringbom, 1987: Ch. 2; Påhlsson, 1983, 1999.)

For more than 600 years Finland belonged to Sweden, until in 1809 Sweden lost Finland to Russia. Then for a little over 100 years Finland was a Grand Duchy of Russia with considerable independence: little in the Swedish constitutional system was changed. Around 1900 the Russians strived to tighten their grip on Finland, but in 1917 the Russian Revolutionary Council agreed to the Finnish plea for independence. Lenin apparently had a soft spot for the country because he had been helped by Finns during his earlier flight through Finland from Russia.

In the decades following Finnish independence, the position of Swedish was debated, sometimes with considerable heat. Eventually, the result was a legislation that is by all standards generous to the rights of the Swedish-speaking minority. Swedish enjoys the status of being the other official language of the country, and Swedish speakers are a well-integrated part of the population. Swedish-speaking Finns can receive their education in their own language from kindergarten to university, and altogether there are 39 Swedish-language secondary schools leading to the Matriculation Examination, preparing them for university studies. Most of the Swedish speakers very definitely consider themselves not as Swedes living in Finland, but as Finns, merely having a different mother tongue from the majority of the population. The English term 'Swedish-speaking Finn' reflects the situation better than the corresponding, traditionally well-established terms in Swedish (*finlandssvensk*) and Finnish (*suomenruotsalainen*). The English term is, however, cumbersome to use and in this volume the terms 'Finns' and 'Swedes' are consistently used for the two language groups in Finland.

Finnish-language and Swedish-language schools in the country have an identical syllabus, and the final examinations leading to university are the same for both groups. Relations between the language groups are good, as is perhaps best evidenced by a steadily increasing number (at present at least 30%) of the students in Swedish-language schools who have Finnish as their L1 or one of the languages spoken at home. Swedish speakers, with the exception of the inhabitants of a few rural areas, generally know Finnish quite well.[4] They simply have to adjust themselves to the use of two languages in their daily life. Thus a large proportion of Swedish-speaking Finns have a bilingual background when learning English, their third language, at school. A point worth emphasising in this context is that their two languages, Swedish and Finnish, are very different both in their structure and in their vocabulary. It seems quite probable that having acquired a good knowledge of a wholly different non-native language widens the linguistic perspective even more than knowledge of two related languages, and thus further facilitates the learning of a third language.

While most Swedish speakers in Finland know Finnish from an early age, Finnish/Swedish bilingualism is relatively rare among Finnish speakers, but when it occurs, they will experience the same advantages as Finland-Swedish bilinguals. The limited contact with Swedish in most parts of the country means that many Finns do not see the need for speaking or learning Swedish. The situation in Finland illustrates Derrick Sharp's (1973: 33) point about a *need not* attitude from a majority language group and a *must* attitude from a minority group. For a long time the Finns' interest in learning other languages has tended to be focused on English.

A new and positive development in the last few decades has been the establishment and increase of a variety of voluntary bilingual and multilingual education programmes in Finnish schools. Some or all of the subjects in a few selected Finnish comprehensive schools are taught in Swedish (less commonly in English). The impetus for this came from Vaasa University, where Christer Laurén and co-workers managed to build up an efficient system (see, for example, Björklund & Suni, 2000). The ideas of immersion-type teaching have caught on, and some schools now have voluntary teaching in English or Swedish. So far, however, this has been restricted to a relatively small number of schools, mainly on the coast, but the results have been encouraging.

The main change that has occurred in Finnish society in recent decades is an increased internationalization, especially in the wake of EU membership 1995. There have, however, been no noticeable changes in the structure of laws and institutions.

Languages have always occupied an important part in the Finnish school curriculum. Before World War II, German had a very strong position, while English was not much studied in Finland. Today, however, the situation is completely different, and the change from German into English as the first foreign language occurred in the 1940s, 1950s and early 1960s. The introduction of the comprehensive school in the late 1970s and 1980s brought further changes in the system. The status of Swedish as an official language of the country had previously been the reason why Swedish was the first non-native language to be introduced in Finnish-language schools. In the present system, the first non-native language is generally introduced in the third year of school when the students are aged 9. The choice of this language is free, but a minimum number of 12 students is required for the language to be taught. The required minimum number for a group choosing a foreign language, however, varies depending on the community and today is often greater than 12. In practice about 90% of the students at Swedish-language schools choose Finnish, while about 90% of the Finnish speakers choose English. This means that throughout school Finnish students have generally studied English for two years longer than Swedish students. If, however, Finnish students choose a language other than Swedish, they will have to read three years of Swedish in their final years of comprehensive school, between the ages of 13 and 16. In Finnish-language schools, up to the mid-1960s, Swedish was still the most frequently studied non-native language. In contrast to the situation then, the present popularity of English in the school system means that Finnish speakers, not least Finns with tertiary education, nowadays tend to know much more English than Swedish. Before the comprehensive school was introduced in the early 1980s, Finns going to university had generally had more Swedish than English at school; but the relative importance of the two languages has now been reversed. Today it is definitely easier to get by with English than with Swedish in those parts of the country (the great majority) where Swedish either is not spoken at all or is spoken by a minority in the community. The level of English teaching at schools in Finland can be considered good, if placed in a wider context: international evaluations of the standard of English in different countries have usually placed Finland at or near the top of the list (see below, pp. 49ff.). Swedish presents a gloomier picture: in recent years it seems clear that the standard of non-native knowledge of Swedish has declined in Finland. An important reason for the recent deterioration of the knowledge of Swedish among Finns with university education is the decreasing number of teaching hours allotted to Swedish at school. The balancing factor of a few Swedish-based bilingual education programmes has so far affected only a small minority of Finnish schools. Mergers of companies and extensive Finnish–Swedish coopera- tion in business and industry have, however, caused many adult Finns at top and middle levels of business administration to improve their medi- ocre school Swedish in order to communicate with partners and customers in Sweden. Though inter-Nordic business is often conducted in English rather than Swedish, Swedish is a more natural language for informal contacts. Finnish is a language hardly known at all in Sweden, although a substantial number of immigrants from Finland and their children keep up Finnish/Swedish bilingualism.

Characteristics of Swedish and Finnish

While Swedish is a Germanic language with a vocabulary and structure very close to Norwegian and Danish, and fairly close to German, Finnish is a Fenno-Ugric language wholly unrelated to the Indo-European language family. The language most closely related to Finnish is Estonian. Hungarian is considered to be a distant relation, though far from comprehensible to a modern Finn. Some loanwords from other languages (traditionally from Swedish, nowadays more from English) have been taken over into Finnish. Such recognisable loans where not only the meaning but also the form has been borrowed are primarily low-frequency words, occurring in academic and professional varieties. Still, even basic international terms in modern society, originally based on Latin or Greek in most European languages, are not transparent to foreigners: telephone is *puhelin* (from *puhua*, 'to speak'), telegraph is *lennätin* (from *lentää*, 'to fly'), restaurant is *ravintola* (from *ravinto*, 'nourishment'). In this respect Finnish has followed the same principles as modern Icelandic: if the foreign word does not fit in with the Finnish phonological and phonotactic system, native elements tend to be used to express the concept. There are fewer phonemes in Finnish than in most European languages: 8 vowels and 13 consonants. A non-Indo-European feature of Finnish is vowel harmony. If the stem of a word has any of the vowels /a/, /o/ or /u/, case endings at the end of the word must also contain the same vowel, but if the stem has no back vowel, the ending will have a front vowel /ä/, /ö/ or /y/ respectively. The inessive case, which is mostly used where English has the preposition 'in', has the variants –*ssa* and –*ssä*. For *talo*, 'house', the meaning 'in the house' is expressed by *talossa*, whereas the corresponding form for 'in the forest', of *metsä*, 'forest' is *metsässä.* Excluding loanwords, Finnish tolerates clusters of consonants only medially, not in initial or final positions in the word.

Morphologically there are considerable differences between Finnish and the Germanic languages. Where Swedish and English use independent words (prepositions, pronouns, auxiliaries, adverbs), Finnish tends to use case endings, verb endings, possessive suffixes or enclitic particles. A striking characteristic of Finnish is its highly developed nominal case system. Foreign learners of Finnish are often taken aback when they hear that there are some 15 cases of the noun in Finnish. The wealth of cases is to some extent balanced by Finnish having extremely few equivalents to English prepositions. A few postpositions occur, but they are not very common either. Relations that in English or Swedish are expressed by prepositions are most commonly rendered by case endings in Finnish, which, however, have other functions as well. In formal Finnish, articles are also lacking as a separate grammatical category. The functions of English articles are generally expressed by other means, often word order. Article-like words, such as *se* 'that' and *yksi* 'one' do, however, occur in colloquial Finnish.

These characteristics make Finnish an agglutinative language, which is able to link a succession of bound morphemes to word stems. As Karlsson (1977) has pointed out, the word as unit contains more semantic information than in English or Swedish – compare the Finnish *talossammekin on uima-allas,* 'our house, too, has a swimming pool' (literally 'in our house, too, is swimming pool').

There is one feature of Finnish that justifies it being called in some way an 'easy' and 'straightforward' language: spelling. Finnish has a highly regular, in fact near-phonemic, orthography with a good correspondence between sound and symbol, at least in formal language. Finns can generally rely on the same symbol always having the same pronunciation, which means that they are not used to differences existing between phonological and orthographic representations of the same word, as is characteristic of English. However, this does not mean that oral and written Finnish are the same. There are differences in choice of both words and word forms between written and ordinary spoken Finnish, but the clear differences are retained when the spoken word is rendered in writing. (*Mä,* 'I' in spoken everyday Finnish, corresponds to *minä* in written and more formal spoken language.) Swedish, on the other hand, resembles English in its comparative irregularity of spelling, although the representation of vowels in particular shows less irregularity than English.

Another regularity in Finnish concerns word stress. Without exception, the stress always falls on the first syllable of the word. This means that Finns are used to linking primary word stress with an immediately preceding word boundary. To them the variable stress in Germanic languages is an unfamiliar phenomenon.

A general problem for learners is how cultural differences are reflected differently in the L1 and the TL. Religious, political and administrative terminology may be too different in the languages for easy word-to-word cross-linguistic equivalences to be accurately established. Within the Western world, these important obstacles to advanced language proficiency are probably not of major significance, at least not in the early stages of learning. Still, there is no doubt that similarities in cultural background will facilitate foreign language learning. The relation between Finnish and Swedish on the one hand and Finnish and English on the other needs some discussion here.

One aspect where Swedish is closer to Finnish than English is concerns vocabulary: how easy it is to establish exact cross-linguistic equivalences. There is a long tradition in Finland of basing loanwords and loan translations into Finnish on Swedish. Finnish and Swedish had the same cultural background for centuries, most conspicuously during the time when Finland was part of Sweden. Cultural, administrative, educational and geographical terms in Finnish thus often have quite close correspondences in Swedish, while one-word equivalences to English may be difficult to find. Swedish influence has had hardly any noticeable effect on the structural characteristics of the Finnish language, but the historical background means that it is possible to point to a purely linguistic reason why Swedish words should be easier to learn for Finns than English words. Classifications of areas of experience are made in similar ways in Finnish and Swedish, whereas English often has a different classification. This means that it is easier to establish close translation equivalents between Finnish and Swedish than between Finnish and English. Such words are more easily learnt than words for which simplified equivalents are hard to establish (Taylor, 1976). Cross-linguistic semantic and conceptual similarity, not only phonological similarity, clearly facilitates anchoring a word in the mental lexicon. There is not much general awareness of this in Finland, and even if there were, it would probably not have much effect on what language Finnish children choose as their first non-native language in school. The choice of this language is in practice determined by pragmatic and political criteria, not linguistic ones, and the position of English as the world language *par preference* today is apparently what decides the issue.

Notes

1. Some badly-needed reappraisals of Lado are Selinker (1992: Ch.1) and Abbott (1983).

2. Errors should not automatically be considered mere indications of shortcomings in learning. The frequent error type *I runned for 'I ran' in children's speech shows that the child has mastered the grammar rule, but has applied it inappropriately.
3. A book that will provide a truly significant step forward in transfer studies is Jarvis & Pavlenko (in press). For the present study, I was not able to make use of this impressive work.
4. The Central Statistical Office in Finland provides an impressive amount of statistics for a large number of research purposes. As far as bilingualism is concerned, however, little material can be found, only statistics for the proportions of different L1s. Different conceptions of what bilingualism actually means may be one reason for this gap. The proportion of bilinguals in 1950 was stated to be 46% for Swedes and 8% for Finns (Sandlund & Björklund, 1980). More recent exact figures for bilinguals are not available. Only after World War II did Finnish become a compulsory subject in all Swedish-language schools. In 1987 I made a rough estimate that at least 75% of Swedish-speaking Finns were able to conduct a conversation in Finnish. If we exclude the Åland Islands, with their internationally-granted special, monolingually-Swedish language status, the percentage of bilinguals in Finland today would probably be around 90%. Depending on the definition, the equivalent figure for bilingualism in Finns today might be, say, 15–20%. The small figure might seem surprising, since practically all educated Finnish speakers have passed the Matriculation Exam in Swedish, which was compulsory up to 2005 and comprises the same types of test as the exam in English. If they are interviewed on Swedish-language radio or television, however, most of them will refuse to speak Swedish and the reporter has to translate from Finnish. The Finns' receptive competence in Swedish is, of course, much better than their production of it.

Chapter 6

Tests of English Comparing Finnish and Swedish Speakers in Finland

The language situation in Finland means that it provides an excellent field for bilingual and multilingual research, and a particularly interesting research area is how Finnish and Finland-Swedish learners differ in their learning of a third language such as English. A lot of material has been gathered in investigations of results achieved in various tests and examinations.[1] These studies can be divided into groups according to the levels tested:

(1) primary schools;
(2) comprehensive schools;
(3) commercial colleges;
(4) Matriculation Examination;
(5) entrance exams;
(6) university students;
(7) international evaluations (IEA, INS).

Primary Schools

There are few comparative studies of the English of Finnish and Finland-Swedish primary school pupils. One reason is that age and introduction of English are not parallel for the language groups: nearly all Finns start to read English in Form 3, at the age of nine, while nearly all Swedish speakers start two years later, in form 5. Two MA theses investigating this level are, however, Sundqvist (1986) and Ekholm (1987). Sundqvist used a translation test L2–L1 in the bilingual town of Pietarsaari/Jakobstad. The subjects had to translate 28 underlined words of an English text. The 41 pupils at the Finnish school had studied English for 3½ years and had had some 270 hours of teaching, while the 64 Swedish pupils had had only 1½ years of English (120 hours of teaching). Yet the Swedish pupils performed better, scoring a mean of 57.9% correct answers as against 53.9% for the Finnish group. A supplementary test in which the subjects had to answer a few simple questions on another English text revealed a slightly greater difference in solution percentage: 74.3% for the Swedes and 67.1% for the Finns.

Ekholm tested 38 Swedish and 39 Finnish 12-year-olds in another bilingual town, Vaasa/Vasa. She focused on translation into L2: the students had to translate an L1-word inserted into an English sentence. Again the Swedish group did better, but only marginally so: the solution percentages were 70.8% for the Swedes and 67.8% for the Finns. The studies by Sundqvist and Ekholm thus showed that, in spite of a smaller number of contact hours, the Swedish speakers had caught up with the Finns, and even surpassed them. Though not too much should be made of the figures in these two fairly restricted studies, it seems that the smaller difference in a production test compared with a comprehension test underscores the implications of Takala's study referred to above (p. 23): the gap between receptive and productive competence is reduced when a target language is perceived to be distant from the L1. The bigger difference in favour of the Swedes in translation from L2 into L1 compared with translation in the opposite direction is explained by cross-linguistic similarities causing a larger 'normal' gap between comprehension and production.

Comprehensive Schools

Some detailed research has been made concerning the level of English at comprehensive school, i.e. students aged 15 at the end of their compulsory schooling. Comprehensive national tests on a voluntary basis are arranged every year at this level, providing a great deal of material for analysis. Two such studies are Ohls-Ahlskog (1995) and Tuokko (2000).

Ohls-Ahlskog analysed the national test of 1993, which comprised listening comprehension, a reaction test, reading comprehension, vocabulary, and a composition. The Swedes ($n = 195$) did better than the Finns ($n = 2156$) in all sections. The mean solution percentage for the Finns was 63%, for the Swedes it was 73%. The biggest differences (more than 10%) were found in the grammar section, in vocabulary and in listening comprehension. Tuokko's analysis of the 1999 test gave almost identical differences in the total results for 5027 Finnish and 614 Swedish speakers. The mean solution percentage for the Finns was 63%, and for the Swedes 74%.

When these results are compared with those of earlier tests at the same level, a considerable improvement in standards can be seen. The general internationalisation of Finland, together with the popularity of English in youth culture, the Internet and other readily available activities outside class, as well as the modernisation of English teaching in the schools are important reasons for this improvement (see below, pp. 108ff.). In Finnish towns it is now generally possible for English-speaking tourists to get along in English in a way that is quite different from the way it was 20 or 30 years ago.

Commercial Colleges

The students at commercial colleges who were the subjects in the studies below had all finished their comprehensive or middle school, but had had little English on top of that. The advantage of testing students at this type of institution is above all that the students come from a large number of different comprehensive schools, which means that the teacher variable can be eliminated.

In a small project in the 1970s that compared 37 Sweden-Swedish, 20 Finland-Swedish and 24 Finnish students, the informants had to read a story aloud and to tell the story of a cartoon in both English and their L1 (Lehtonen, 1979, summarised in Ringbom, 1987: 89f.). There were considerable differences in the free speech of the groups. The total rate of English speech (but not L1 speech) of the Finns was lower and the percentage of pauses higher, the pauses often being placed in a way that broke the normal constituent structure of the sentence. The result for the Finns was staccato speech with disturbing pauses. The Finland-Swedish subjects were more fluent, but not as fluent as the Sweden Swedes, who, however made a very large number of spelling errors in their writing. The results can largely be referred to the negligence of oral foreign language skills in Finland at that time – in Sweden the oral skills had already gained a much more prominent place in language teaching classrooms.

Another early study was made by Granfors and Palmberg (1976), who studied 42 Finland-Swedish and 58 Finnish students at a commercial college in Vaasa. One task was to retell the story of a cartoon, the other to translate a short text into English. The study focused on article errors, preposition errors and concord errors. A special device was to make use of an actual/potential error index, which made for acceptable accuracy in frequencies also for the story telling. Every noun or noun phrase in the text that could be preceded by an article, a numeral or possessive pronoun, as well as every word that could not be preceded by an article but in the material still did was regarded as a potential article error. The proportion of actual errors committed compared with potential errors could then be calculated in the form of an actual/potential error index. The higher the index, the more errors have occurred. The results can be seen in Table 1.

Articles and prepositions are, of course, especially problematic for Finns, as is frequently pointed out by anybody teaching English in Finland.

Table 1 Mean actual/potential error index for commercial college students

a/p index for	Articles		Prepositions		Concord	
	story	translation	story	translation	story	translation
Finns (n = 58)	8.1	7.7	16.6	23.4	2.4	6.4
Swedes (n = 42)	3.5	2.1	10.3	11.5	1.0	2.7

The Matriculation Examination

The annual National Matriculation Examination in Finland, a standard-ised test for 19-year-old school leavers aiming to go on to university-level studies, provides a great deal of further material. A very large number of students, about 30,000, take the exam every spring and detailed statistics are available from the Examination Board.[2] Until the late 1970s, the exam consisted only of translation from and into the foreign language. (For a comparative analysis of one such test, see Nurmi, 1988. Figures for the listening comprehension and reading comprehension tests up to 1989 can be seen in Ringbom, 1992: 96.) From the 1980s onwards, the exam has always comprised at least listening comprehension, reading comprehen-sion and an essay. In the 1990s a multiple choice cloze test was introduced, where both vocabulary and grammar were tested. Table 2 shows the results of the multiple choice parts of listening comprehension, reading compre-hension and the Cloze test for the last 14 years.

The differences in favour of the Swedes are consistent and can be seen from Table 3, which was compiled from Table 2. This shows that the consis-tently greatest differences occur in the multiple choice cloze test, where the difference each year exceeds 10%. It also indicates that the Finns' problems with grammar and vocabulary, which were in the foreground also at the earlier stage of comprehensive school, are still considerable. With the exception of four years, the figures for listening comprehension are higher than the figures for reading comprehension. This was also the case for each year between 1980 and 1989 (Ringbom, 1992: 91).

The mean total score of the exam in English is also always higher for Swedish schools than for Finnish ones. In 1998 out of a maximum of 299 points, the figures were 250 for Swedes and 226 for Finns (Sajavaara & Takala, 2000: 189). The total score of the exam in English for the last three years can be seen from Table 4, which shows the percentual distribution of the different marks in English.

Table 2 Mean solution percentages in the multiple choice sections of the Matriculation Examination (Spring exam in English)

	Finnish schools (n = 391,823)			Swedish schools (n = 24,610)		
	Listening compreh.	*Reading compreh.*	*MC cloze*	*Listening compreh.*	*Reading compreh.*	*MC cloze*
1991	76.8	72.7	69.8	87.3	81.8	81.2
1992	78.2	79.3	72.8	89.3	86.8	86.8
1993	80.0	71.2	77.2	87.3	79.2	87.6
1994	73.5	80.5	63.7	79.5	89.0	80.0
1995	86.5	78.5	65.3	90.0	85.5	78.8
1996	83.0	74.0	70.9	90.0	85.2	82.4
1997	78.5	69.0	66.0	86.5	77.0	78.8
1998	74.5	83.5	78.5	83.0	89.0	90.0
1999	77.5	71.0	69.0	87.0	77.0	79.3
2000	70.2	77.9	65.1	80.4	82.5	78.1
2001	68.8	72.3	64.7	77.8	78.7	78.4
2002	68.0	72.0	68.9	74.7	78.0	79.8
2003	79.0	71.2	65.2	86.6	77.2	78.5
2004	73.3	73.2	58.4	80.6	78.0	73.2

The percentage of failures pinpoints the difference between the language groups: 0.3% of the candidates from Swedish schools (just 5 candidates) fail the exam in English, while the percentage of failures in Finnish schools is ten times larger. The three highest marks are consistently achieved by a considerably larger proportion of Swedish candidates. If one looks at the best candidates in the exam, however, each year there are a small number of candidates from both language groups who write excellent essays of a native-like standard, and whose multiple choice tests are equivalent or almost equivalent to native speaker standards. But the scale of proficiency is extremely varied in Finnish schools: the essays produced by the weakest candidates are very poor with limited vocabulary and overly simple constructions, and with bad errors occurring in almost every sentence. Clearly 7 to 10 years of English teaching does *not* automatically

Table 3   Differences in mean solution percentages between Finnish and Swedish schools

	Reading comprehension	*Listening comprehension*	*Multiple choice cloze*
1991	9.1	10.5	11.4
1992	7.5	11.1	14.0
1993	8.0	7.3	10.4
1994	8.5	6.0	16.3
1995	7.0	3.5	13.5
1996	11.2	7.0	11.5
1997	8.0	8.0	12.8
1998	5.5	8.5	11.5
1999	6.0	9.5	10.3
2000	4.6	10.2	13.0
2001	6.4	9.0	13.7
2002	6.0	6.7	10.9
2003	6.0	7.6	13.3
2004	4.8	7.3	14.8

lead to adequate proficiency in every learner. Even among candidates taking the Matriculation Examination, it is justified to talk about advanced, intermediate and weak levels of proficiency.

Meriläinen (2006) has analysed the lexical L1-transfer errors made by Finns in the Matriculation Exam in 1990 and in 2000. About half of the errors in her corpus (some 60,000 words) are semantic extensions, loan translations, collocational errors and prepositional errors. The other half includes orthographic errors (such as the use of lower case rather than upper case letters), grammatical errors and language shifts. Errors due to formal cross-linguistic similarity are extremely rare. They occur in some orthographical errors, mainly in loanwords, such as *traktor* for 'tractor' (Finnish: *traktori*). Meriläinen also gives an example from her own teaching experience where a student at an early stage of learning said 'I mean drown' and explained that she was basing this on the Finnish equivalent '*minä meinasin hukkua*'. The Finnish verb *meinata* most commonly = 'mean', but in this case = 'be about to'.

Table 4 Percentual distribution of the marks awarded for English in the Matriculation Examination

	L	E	M	C	B	A	Fail
2002:							
Finnish schools (*n* = 28,540)	5.1	15.2	19.9	22.9	22.4	11.6	2.9
Swedish schools (*n* = 1486)	7.7	22.8	30.5	25.4	11.4	1.9	0.3
2003:							
Finnish schools (*n* = 27,535)	4.8	16.6	21.0	23.8	20.6	10.2	3.0
Swedish schools (*n* = 1584)	8.8	28.3	30.9	21.1	9.4	1.2	0.3
2004:							
Finnish schools (*n* = 26,768)	4.7	17.0	21.0	23.7	20.4	10.1	3.0
Swedish schools (*n* = 1457)	8.4	28.3	30.0	22.2	9.4	1.4	0.3

Note: The pass marks, from highest to lowest, are L (*laudatur*), E (*eximia cum laude*), M (*magna cum laude*), C (*cum laude*), B (*lubenter*) and A (*approbatur*)

Other languages than English, above all German, are also included in the Matriculation Exam, mostly on a voluntary basis. Comparisons have shown the expected result that Swedish schools do consistently better in German than Finnish schools do (Sajavaara & Takala, 2000: 189).

University Entrance Exams

Only 50–60% of those passing the Matriculation Examination in the 1970s and 1980s could count on being admitted to studies at a traditional university in Finland. (Recently, in Finland as in Britain, the upgrading of polytechnics to university status has raised the percentage of university students.) From the 1950s onwards, English studies at university level have been popular (more so than other subjects in the humanities), and the number of applicants to English departments at all Finnish universities has consistently been much higher than those accepted. The screening has been carried out mainly by an entrance exam. Of those applying for a place at the

Åbo Akademi English Department (about 100 each year), between 30 and 50% were Finnish speakers in the 1970s and 1980s. After that, problems in arranging the compulsory didactic training aimed at teaching in Finnish-language schools reduced the number of Finnish applicants to a mere trickle, which meant that only earlier entrance exams to Åbo Akademi can provide meaningful comparisons of Finnish and Swedish speakers.

Studies of entrance exams are Wahlman-Tyrsky (1976), M. Sjöholm (1979), and R. Suomi (1984). They all present more or less the same picture: Swedish speakers do better, but the differences are generally not as clear as in investigations of school-level English. The main differences concern the use of articles and prepositions, which still pose greater problems to Finns than to Swedes. Tables showing the results of the different sections of the entrance exams from 1975 to 1978 are given by Ringbom (1987: 83).

In some years in the 1970s, a sound recognition test and a partial dictation test were included in the entrance exam. The sound recognition test revealed very minor differences between Finns and Swedish Finns (Ringbom, 1987: 83), but the partial dictation revealed some interesting differences, as shown by M. Sjöholm (1979). The words showing the greatest differences in solution percentage were *to* (53.5% difference in favour of the Swedes), *in* (46.8%), *'d* (40.7%), *of* (35.3%), *the* (32.2%) and *him* (30.0%). These words occurred in the contexts *advantage of the apostle, he'd bragged to Dawson,* and *it'd be made up to him in other ways.* The confusion caused by the low-frequency words *apostle* and *bragged* is reflected much less in the solution percentages for the words themselves than in the high-frequency words in their immediate environment (cf. Ringbom, 1987: 84ff.).

University Students

Some studies have focused on the difference between students at departments of English and students reading other subjects. Lindros (1987) is a comparative study of communicative apprehension while speaking English. In part, Lindros reproduced and made use of the results of a Jyväskylä study (Lehtonen *et al.*, 1985). Students who read political science at Jyväskylä University were found to be much more apprehensive than their peers at Åbo Akademi, while this difference did not exist for students of English at these universities (see below, p.114 n. 3). Påhlsson (1983: 63) also strongly emphasises the much more pronounced willingness of Swedish Finns to use English orally and states that 'the existence of such a difference will have to be acknowledged by anyone with teaching experience from both Finnish and Swedish schools'.

Similarly, in a vocabulary test, where care had been taken not to include any English words similar to Swedish, Wernér (1995) showed that the students of English at Åbo Akademi and at the Finnish-language Turku University were on the same level, but that Swedish speakers reading other university subjects scored higher than Finnish students. Back (1992) studied students in Vaasa/Vasa reading for a translator's exam (Finnish-Swedish or Swedish-Finnish). Again the Finns made more errors in their English than the Swedes.

Påhlsson (1983, 1999) made detailed studies of the English of students at the Swedish School of Economics in Helsinki (Svenska Handelshögskolan). He used Zettersten's (1979) test of the receptive English vocabulary of Nordic students of English, where Finnish as well as Finland-Swedish (Åbo Akademi) students were seen to lag behind their Swedish, Norwegian and Danish colleagues. The difference between students of English and students at the School of Economics was, however, considerable in favour of the university students. Engberg (1993) used Zettersten's test as one of her two vocabulary tests and found that the standard for Åbo Akademi first-year students of English at university level had not changed noticeably in 15 years.

Elo (1993) compared the students of French at the Finnish-language Turku University and the Swedish-language Åbo Akademi University. At that time there was not advanced teaching of French at Åbo Akademi, but by special arrangements the Åbo students could move over to Turku University after a few introductory courses. Most university students of French have had only a couple of years of French at school, which means that they are far from being at the same proficiency level as students of English. The Åbo Akademi students obtained regularly better results in proficiency tests in French.

International Evaluations

In the international IEA study of 1971 (Lewis & Massad, 1975), only Finnish-language schools in Finland took part. This international project comparing the standard of English was conducted in the pre-comprehensive school days, when translation from and into foreign languages was the only test type in the Matriculation Examination, and any classroom deviation from the grammar–translation-based method in language teaching was up to the individual teacher. In most countries the situation was probably rather similar. The countries participating in the project were Belgium, Chile, Federal Republic of Germany, Finland, Hungary, Israel, Italy, Holland, Sweden and Thailand. The Finns' results were summarised in the following way: the Finnish 18-year-olds at upper secondary school were 'first in grammar, second in writing and listening comprehension, third in speaking and fourth in reading comprehension' (Takala & Havola, 1983: 24).

The text used for the IEA multiple-choice reading comprehension test was also used in Finland in 1979 and 1983 (Linnakylä & Saari, 1993), and considerable improvement could be found. Thus, while the mean solution percentage in 1971 was 57.1, it had increased to 66.9% in 1979 and 75.2% in 1983. Following the IEA study, the communicative aspects of language teaching began to be stressed. The changes in foreign language teaching in Finland can be linked to the introduction of the comprehensive school in the 1970s. Test types other than translation came into use, as did tapes and tape-recorders. When test items in the IEA listening-comprehension test were used again in 1991, the 16-year-olds in comprehensive schools understood English sentences as well as the 19-year-old school leavers 20 years before (Sajavaara & Takala, 2000: 186).

An international investigation of English proficiency at school in 2002 focused on the same age group as the IEA study (Bonnet, 2004). The Finnish subjects came from both Finnish-language and Swedish-language schools. The other countries participating were Denmark, France, Holland, Norway, Spain and Sweden. Norway and Sweden had the best results, with a mean solution percentage of 68. Finland had 61%,[3] Holland 61%, Denmark 59%, Spain 45% and France 36%. A full description of this project can be found on the website of the *European Network*. The tests used were listening comprehension, grammar, reading comprehension and writing, and there were few noticeable differences between these sections. The Swedish schools in Finland attained higher results in all the test types than the Finnish schools. If we, however, compare the Finnish results with schools from other countries, there is a consistent improvement for Finns in comparison with the previous IEA study 25 years earlier. This can be explained partly by the changes in language teaching, partly by the internationalisation that has changed Finland more thoroughly than the other participating countries, whose foreign contacts in the 1970s and before were already much more extensive.

A significant background factor is that the motivation for learning English is high in Finland: 90% of the pupils participating in the 2002 study reported liking the subject to some extent or very much (Tuokko, 2003: 5).

The most recent comparative international study is the INS study, which primarily investigates comprehension of the Scandinavian neighbour languages, but which also gave a comprehension test of English to teenagers in the Nordic countries. Again the Finnish-language schools did better than their Danish peers, though not as well as the Swedes, Norwegians and Finland-Swedish students. The last mentioned were marginally top of the list.

Studies by Non-Finnish Researchers

The language situation in Finland has not been investigated by many researchers from abroad. However, one who has done so is Scott Jarvis, who made good use of his knowledge of both Finnish and Swedish in his 1997 Indiana University PhD thesis. Jarvis deals with the semantic-conceptual aspects of L1 transfer on Finnish and Finland-Swedish learners' word choice in English. Methodologically Jarvis' work is at a high level and in his comparative evaluation of the standards of the two language groups (Jarvis, 1999) he arrives at very much the same results as Finnish researchers. The importance of the conceptual base of L1 for L2 vocabulary choice is firmly established, being manifested in pervasive L1 influence in lexical use. In a recent paper together with Terence Odlin (Jarvis & Odlin, 2000), Jarvis has further used his material to show how Finnish and Finland-Swedish learners are influenced by their L1 in their choice of locative and directional English expressions. Finnish learners make cross-linguistic identifications between the post-posed bound morphology of their L1 and the pre-posed free morphology of English prepositions (see below, pp. 67ff.).

Differences between Finnish and Swedish Learners of English

From all the studies that compare Finnish-speaking and Swedish-speaking learners of English, one conclusion is obvious: Swedish speakers have a great advantage in learning English. From the outset they can rely on their L1 for essential facilitation of learning. This advantage also applies to the learning of French (Elo, 1993) and German (Sajavaara & Takala, 2000: 189). Swedes make a much smaller number of errors at various levels. The difference is particularly conspicuous at early stages of learning when they can immediately recognise and understand a sizable number of English words – compare the studies quoted above (p. 11) investigating how much English Swedish-speaking and Finnish-speaking children can understand before they start to learn the language at school.

In practice, the positive transfer effect of having a mother tongue related to the target language is more significant than a few more years of English at school. But a trend that can be seen is that the higher the proficiency level, the smaller the difference, which disappears altogether in students reading English as a university subject (i.e. future teachers of English). The development illustrates the decreasing importance of positive L1 transfer when proficiency improves. It is also noticeable that there has been considerable improvement in English proficiency in schools over the last 20–30 years and that this improvement is most obvious in Finnish students. The standards of Swedish schools in Finland have also gone up, but, it seems, not as much.

The essential reasons for the differences between Swedes and Finns must be sought in the linguistic differences between Finnish and Swedish (cf. Ringbom, 1987: Ch. 7). From their L1, Swedish speakers are familiar with and do not have to spend effort on learning the functions and use of such grammatical categories as articles and prepositions. At the early stages of learning, Finnish speakers, on the other hand, will have difficulties in establishing cross-linguistic one-to-one equivalences to their L1. They have to grapple with the basic organisational problem of making sense of a linguistic system that in parts is foreign to their habitual mode of linguistic reasoning. The structural similarities between English and Finnish are insignificant compared with those between Swedish and English. It is difficult for Finnish learners to perceive them and they probably need to be explicitly pointed out to learners for facilitation to occur. The phonological differences between English and Finland-Swedish also exist between English and Finnish, but in addition there are differences between Finnish and English that do not exist between English and Finland-Swedish. A considerable learning problem for Finns is the fortis/lenis distinction between stops in the Germanic languages.

> It is well known to anyone involved in teaching English to Finnish students that it is difficult for Finns to distinguish between English /p t k/ and /b d g/ and that, in addition to minor phonetic mistakes, many phonemic ones occur, both in production and in perception. (K. Suomi, 1976: 1)

As for the Swedes' consistently greater advantage in listening comprehension compared with reading comprehension, see p. 45.

In lexis, the frequent cognates with English that are characteristic of Swedish can be contrasted with the non-Indo-European character of Finnish basic vocabulary. It is not difficult for Swedes to convert their potential lexical knowledge to real receptive knowledge where a number of primary counterparts are established. This can be contrasted with the lack of formal similarities between Finnish and English high-frequency items

The summary above has focused on differences, but it may be necessary to emphasise once more that the reason why the two language groups differ is first and foremost a question of presence vs. lack of similarities: absence of positive transfer for the Finnish learner.

Notes

1. Many comparative studies of Finnish and Finland-Swedish learners have been carried out in the English Department at Åbo Akademi University. They are mostly unpublished MA theses, where a variety of material has been collected. Nearly all the authors are now practicing English teachers in schools in Finland, few of them having gone on to further research for the licentiate or doctorate. Seen in a wider perspective, the data in these studies are fairly limited, and what some of them understandably enough lack is a deeper realisation of how their results could be relevant to the broader picture of foreign language learning. Nor do all the studies provide very extensive linguistic background. Nonetheless, the collection and analysis of the material has generally been carried out with great care, and in their own way these studies have made a contribution to the field of transfer research. Their results conform well with each other and with other research

2. I am grateful to Samuli Wilkman of the National Examination Board for providing the statistics of the Matriculation Exams.

3. 10% of the Finnish material came from Swedish-language schools. Their mean solution percentage was 75 while the percentage for the Finnish schools was 59% (Tuokko, 2003: 15).

Chapter 7

Levels of Transfer: Items and Procedures (Systems)

Item Transfer, Procedural Transfer and Overall Transfer

The use of cross-linguistic similarities, i.e. transfer, can be manifested at three different levels: (1) item level, (2) system level, and (3) overall level. The distinction between items and systems sheds light on one of the basic questions in transfer research, what is actually transferred.[1]

Cruttenden (1981) first made the distinction between item learning and system learning, relating to L1 acquisition. Before systems can be learned, a number of items have to be known. Item learning 'involves a form which is uniquely bonded with some other form or with a unique referent, whereas system-learning involves the possibility of the commutation of forms or referents while some (other) form is held constant' (Cruttenden, 1981: 79). This distinction can be usefully applied to SLA as well. The unique bondage characteristic of item learning is predominantly cross-linguistic, since the relevant concepts already exist in the (adult) learner's mind.

Initially, learning takes place on an item-by-item basis in all areas of language: phonological, morphological, syntactic, lexical and phrase-ological. Thus, items in item transfer are not only words, lexical items, they can just as well be phonemes, morphemes, syntactic units or phrases. In production, memorisation of chunks of 'survival language' may aid the beginning learner, as when the tourist with a minimal foreign language competence has concentrated on learning useful phrases from his guide-book, such as 'Where is the toilet?' or 'How do I get to the railway station?'[2]

In the closed systems of phonology and morphology, the learner does not normally dwell very long at the stage of item learning, at least not if he can fall back on some kind of reference frame. In the open system of lexis, on the other hand, both item learning and system learning are important throughout: learning both new lexical items and the complex ways in which old and new items are linked to other items provides a challenge at all stages of learning.

54

The underlying similarities of item transfer (a roughly corresponding term used by Corder (1983) being *borrowing*) are a concretely perceived similarity of form and an associated, assumed similarity of function or meaning between source language and target language. It has a predominantly positive effect on learning, notably on learning for comprehension. Learners make use of an oversimplified equivalence hypothesis, L2 = L1, mapping the functions or meanings of L2 items directly on to existing L1 items in comprehension and those of L1 items on to L2 items in production. This is the case particularly at low levels of learning, when the learner's linguistic resources in L2 are insufficient to make extended use of intralingual similarities. Simplified cross-linguistic one-to-one relationships are established to reduce the learner's workload. At early learning stages, learners tend to focus on form rather than on the more abstract concepts of meaning or function, and perceived formal similarities aid them in establishing cross-linguistic relations in long-term memory.

Perceived similarity of form, combined with an assumed similarity of meaning, provides the basis for establishing a simplified one-to-one relation between an L2 item and an L1 item, finding 'primary counterparts' to use Arabski's term (1979). Andersen (1984) also discusses 'the one-to-one principle of interlanguage construction'. In system transfer, on the other hand, abstract principles of organising information in L1 are transferred. For system transfer, a better term might be *procedural transfer*. Other terms used are 'similarity of principle' (Rogers, 1997), and 'imposition of higher-level rules' (Albert & Obler, 1978: 211). Positive procedural transfer lies behind the easy comprehension of a related target language, although it is not easy to point to concrete evidence for it. It assumes cross-linguistic functional equivalence while formal item similarity is normally not involved. An example will elucidate this. One Finnish word, *kieli*, has two separate meanings, 'language' and 'tongue'. This L1 organising principle is applied to L2 production of English, which uses two different words. The learner knows only one of these (usually the prototypical and/or the more frequent one), and uses it for both meanings, 'he bit himself in the language'. The difference between learning a related language vs. an unrelated one is largely whether the principles used for organising the L1 can also be applied to the L2. In procedural transfer the learner incorporates a productive mechanism, applying L1-based principles to L2. In transfer of procedures no formal cross-linguistic similarities need to be perceived for transfer to occur. Procedural transfer is nearly always transfer from L1, or possibly another language the learner knows very well, but a language the learner knows only superficially does not generally give rise to procedural transfer (see below, pp. 78ff.). Apparently grammatical rules and semantic properties must be well internalised, preferably automatised, in order to be transferred. Since functional and semantic systems in two languages are hardly ever fully congruent, procedural transfer in production tends to lead to error, and thus nearly always has a negative effect (though the difficulty of recognising positive effects of transfer in both comprehension and production must be reckoned with). The learner's tendency to assume one-to-one cross-linguistic relationships is frequently in conflict with the actual network of one-to-many or many-to-many relations in the real world. Vocabulary learning after a basic item-learning stage includes both system learning (qualitative) and item learning (mainly quantitative).

Inevitable oversimplifications in item learning will be modified as learning progresses. Lowie and Verspoor also make this point:

> At initial stages of L2 acquisition, a full overlap may be assumed between the conceptual representations of the L1 learner and the L2 learner. Gradually, the differences between the L1 and the L2 lemma will be acquired, which may eventually lead to a 'native-like' lexical representation. (Lowie & Verspoor, 2004: 80)

Learning systems is always preceded by learning items, and system learning involves a gradual modification of the oversimplified one-to-one relations of item learning. The learner gradually reaches a stage where s/he can see which shade of meaning of a word is most suitable to the context where it occurs.

R. Ellis (1995: 311f.), among others, makes the important point that 'the absence of a structural feature in the L1 may have as much impact on the L2 as the presence of a different feature'. The procedural transfer that learners use in production is of two kinds, intrusive and inhibitive (Hammerly, 1991: 63). Intrusive transfer leads to inappropriate use of L1-based items and structures, inhibitive transfer prevents or inhibits learning to use new words and structures appropriately. Inhibitive transfer occurs when the learner's L1 does not have specific structures of the TL and it tends to be manifested as underuse or avoidance in production (cf. Kleinmann, 1977). (Strictly speaking, nothing is actually transferred, so in this case 'cross-linguistic influence' might be a more appropriate term. Transfer and cross-linguistic influence are, however, used interchangeably in this volume.) TL words and structures that have no parallel in L1 provide the learner with no concrete basis for positive item transfer and are therefore often avoided. Avoidance may imply that a particular structure is *known* (i.e. can be passively recognised) by learners, but not freely *used* by them (cf. Levenston, 1971).

Overall transfer is an umbrella term, relying on both formal similarity of individual items and to what extent there is functional equivalence between the underlying systems. It depends on how much cross-linguistic similarity the learner can generally perceive between items and systems in the two languages, beginning from a common alphabet, phonemes in common and similar phonotactics, over the division into grammatical categories (case, gender, word classes) to the number of cognates and other lexical similarities. It is particularly evident in comprehension and has a general facilitating effect on learning, explaining why a language related to the L1 can be mastered in a much shorter time than an unrelated one. In SLA literature, references can be found to estimates by British or American authorities of how long it takes for English speakers to learn various languages (Corder, 1979: 27; Odlin, 1989: 39ff.; Ringbom, 1987: 66). These estimates, obviously made by competent professionals, have, for instance, determined different rates of language proficiency allowance for members of the British Foreign Service.

Item transfer in comprehension is overwhelmingly positive: if cross-linguistic similarities between items can be perceived and established, comprehension is facilitated. Quick and effective item learning for comprehension is above all what distinguishes the learning of a related TL from learning an unrelated language. As for procedural transfer in comprehension, the matter is more complex. Learners normally assume that L1 procedures work also for L2 comprehension. The extent to which these assumptions actually work determines whether the effect is positive or negative. Any positive, facilitating effects are, however, hard for the researcher to spot. If inappropriate L1 procedures are applied to L2 comprehension, misinterpretations are likely to arise, especially in listening comprehension. When learners realise that some L1 procedures actually do not work for L2 comprehension, they are likely to be confused. Like procedural transfer in production, procedural transfer in comprehension is thus concretely seen as having a predominantly negative effect. In listening comprehension, for example, L1 rules for discerning word boundaries may not work. Or L2 may not have the same phonotactic L1 constraints, such as the Finnish intolerance of consonant clusters at the beginning or end of words. In grammar, syntactic congruence has a key role: if the L2 has categories absent from the L1, the functions of these have to be learnt for comprehension to occur. Across closely-related languages, none of this poses much of a problem: L1 procedures are fairly appropriate and tend to work well for comprehension. What is important for learners is to reach a stage of knowing a sufficient number of items (words). Then approximate comprehension generally works.

There are, however, differences between reading comprehension and listening comprehension.

Similarities in Reading vs. Similarities in Listening

Learners make use of cross-linguistic similarities in comprehension, but the differences between listening and reading affect the use of these similarities differently (see, for example, Koster, 1987; Reves & Levine, 1988). By self-study, learning a fair number of words in the TL, it is relatively easy to acquire a reasonable reading competence in a closely-related language, such as Dutch for a Swedish speaker. However, to understand what people actually say to you is a different matter. The difference between standard language and regional dialects is part of the problem, but hardly the most essential reason for the difficulties that a fairly proficient reader encounters in real oral situations. The main problems are more likely to be due to the general differences between spoken and written language. These differences are certainly considerable in languages such as English and French.

Teaching may have made a learner perfectly familiar with a particular item in writing, but s/he may be unable to recognise its spoken form. Not all speech elements are precisely identified in listening. If words are written or spoken in isolation, they have a certain stability, but when they occur in connected speech they exhibit a great deal of variation. Sounds may be slurred and cardinal vowels may be reduced. English is a particularly tricky language in that the relation between phonological and orthographic representations of words is very complex, especially in its vowel system. One symbol can represent many sounds, and one sound can be expressed by many symbols. The segmentation of speech into words often poses problems for the untrained L2 listener, who is frequently uncertain where a word begins and where it ends. Extra-linguistic features (such as situational context, gestures and tone of voice) that aid successful oral communication are far from always sufficient to compensate for the problems facing somebody listening to a language that is very distant from his/her L1. In oral communication, reliance on form does not help the listener as much as it aids the reader, whose task will be more concretely aided by perceived similarities between words. In L2 reading, lexical knowledge, both actual and potential, will aid the reader considerably, partly because the reader has more time at his disposal than a listener has.

The subskills of reading are similar to those of listening, but, in the words of Reves and Levine (1988: 335), listening is 'a more integrated, less divisible skill, in which the unitary skill factor is more dominant than the composite parts of the skill'. In listening, subskills 'tend to cumulatively contribute to a holistic comprehension of the message' (Reves &Levine, 1988: 334). Perceived lexical similarities do not affect listening as much as they affect reading: the stimuli of oral L2 input apparently do not activate formally similar L1 items as easily as do the clearly set out words of a written text. Also, the learner might be more familiar with the written than the spoken form of the word. The more holistic approach to listening means that the potential lexical knowledge that a learner has will be of less direct use than it is for reading. In reading a related L2, there will be much (positive) item transfer based on formal cross-linguistic similarity between words.

Listening is not as much facilitated by lexical item transfer, with its essentially positive effects, but the L2 listener will apply to the L2 those procedures developed for L1. How similar the L1 and L2 procedures are largely determines whether or not comprehension is facilitated, whether or not there will be positive transfer. The key question is: To what extent do L1-procedures work for L2? Application of L1 procedures to L2 is made at a subconscious level, and when it works it is difficult to observe from outside. Unless the languages concerned are very close, procedural transfer generally has a negative effect and prevents the development of automaticity in L2. Automaticity is much more important to listening than it is to reading, because of the constant time constraints in oral communication.

The following alternative questions can then be put, relating to comparisons of learners of a related vs. an unrelated language:

(1) Does a lower amount of positive item transfer in listening over reading lead to a reduced advantage for learners with a related L1 in a listening comprehension test compared with a reading test?
(2) Or do the additional problems of listening and the lack of positive transfer cause an increased difference in listening compared with reading?

Answers can be found in a comparison of the listening and reading comprehension sections in the Finnish Matriculation Exam given above (pp. 45ff.). Since the difference in the listening comprehension part is consistently higher in favour of the Swedes than the difference in the reading comprehension part, it seems clear that there are additional problems with listening that affect Finns more than Swedes. The greater distance between Finnish and English, compared to that between Swedish and English, means that Finns have more difficulties in achieving automaticity: the time pressure of an oral situation poses more obstacles to Finns. There are also features of the Finnish language that Germanic languages do not have, and there are features common to the Germanic languages that Finnish does not have (see above, p. 37 and Ringbom, 1987: 87ff.).

Since the primary word stress in Finnish always falls on the first syllable, Finns are used to associating word stress with a preceding word boundary, a principle that does not work for English. The variable word stress in English confuses the Finnish learner whose L1 has features (such as vowel harmony and the absence of word initial and word final clusters of consonants) that further accentuate word boundaries. It is also relevant that the word in Finnish has a more important status as a linguistic unit (i.e. it contains more information) than it does in English or Swedish. The analysis of partial dictation tests shows that Finns often leave unstressed prefixes and function words without attention in contexts where the vocabulary poses special difficulties. Finns sometimes cannot perceive the first unstressed syllable of an English word. Meriläinen (2006: 88) gives examples of errors made in the writing of English compositions in the Matriculation Exam: the production of *creasing* pro 'increasing' and *the mount of people* pro 'the amount of people'. Compared with reading tests, there is a greater difference in favour of the Swedes between the two language groups in listening comprehension tests, both the multiple choice type used in the Matriculation Exam and partial dictation. This must be seen against the different effects of time constraints in oral situations. Apparently Swedish learners have been able to automatise their receptive knowledge more efficiently than the Finns: they can retrieve it with more speed and accuracy (see further below, pp. 90f.). Swedish learners are used to variable stress, since word stress in their L1, as in English, is generally, but not always, on the first syllable.

Notes

1. Different use of the terms item and system is made by R. Ellis (1999).
2. Not every 'useful' phrase in guidebooks of an early date ('parlours') is all that helpful, as the well-known example 'the postilion has been struck by lightning' indicates. I have come across a guidebook for Sweden from the 19th century where the list of useful phrases includes (in translation) 'the monkey has torn its chain and bitten the maid in her cheekbone'.

Chapter 8

Item Transfer in Production: Areas of Language

Comparative investigations of oral production pose special problems for both language testing and research. When Finnish and Finland-Swedish production of English is dealt with below, it is written production that has been analysed. There are plans to introduce oral production in the Finnish Matriculation Exam, but so far practical problems have prevented it. The only comparative investigation of Finnish and Finland-Swedish oral production dates back to the 1970s, when Lehtonen (1979) made a small-scale comparison of Finnish, Finland-Swedish and Sweden-Swedish learners at the commercial college level. Information about the results can also be found in Ringbom (1987: 82ff.).

The tests were made before the changes of teaching methods had been introduced in Finland. Lehtonen analysed speech rate and pauses, and he uses careful phrasing about any differences found. In his conclusion he makes the following points:

> The total rate of speech of Finnish-speaking Finns is dramatically lower and the percentage of pauses higher than those of Swedish-speaking Finns and Swedes ... In addition to the pause time and the total rate of speech, the articulation rate of the Finns' English is also lower than that of the speakers in the other groups. (Lehtonen, 1979: 49)

Compared with Finland-Swedish speakers, Finns tended to produce less fluent, staccato speech with many pauses, also in places where pauses do not occur in native speech.

Selective use of L1 knowledge and procedures appears in all language areas. When this occurs and leads to accurate native-like production, it is not easy to discern the underlying positive transfer. Negative transfer, on the other hand, as manifested in, for example, syntactic errors and use of false cognates can be linked to the L1 without difficulty. But L1 influence can be manifested also in other ways.

Inhibitive procedural transfer can be manifested as avoidance or underproduction (see Dagut & Laufer, 1985; Ijaz, 1986; Laufer & Eliasson, 1993; K. Sjöholm, 1995). There is, however, another reason for avoidance or underuse of particular idioms or words with non-core meanings: the learner's intuition that they are language-specific to L1 (Kellerman, 1978).

The extent of transfer varies, depending on many other variables of SLA. Relevant are at least the following: stage of learning, mode of learning, input, social setting and individual learner features (aptitude, age, meta-linguistic awareness, literacy, language proficiency, language anxiety, use of strategies, educational and social background). The complex interaction of transfer with these variables is still not much understood and it cannot be dealt with here. In the following sections I will consider the extent of transfer as it appears in phonology, discourse and pragmatics, grammar, and lexis.

Phonology

Evidence of L1 transfer is clearly seen in the area of phonology. It has, however, always been shown to be negative transfer, as positive phonological transfer has not been studied in any depth, as far as I know. Learners initially perceive L2 sounds in terms of the phonological system of the L1 (Eckman, 2004: 521). Even learners who are able to speak and write another language fluently generally retain a foreign accent. As learners' L1 clearly influences the acquisition of L2 phonology, the original predictions of contrastive analysis (CA) may seem to work fairly well at the phonological level, at least on the surface. If there are numerous mutually-exclusive forms and patterns between L1 and L2, this will cause obstacles to the learner's rapid achievement of reasonable oral competence. The closed system of phonology lends itself best to systematic contrastive analysis, and many, though not all, learner problems can be referred back to the L1 background. In general terms, great phonological differences mean learning difficulties at the outset of learning. A foreign accent is more clearly manifested in the early stages than in the later stages of learning (see for example, Major, 1987). At first learners have a very low competence in the target language: in rhythm, in stress and intonation, and in individual speech sounds, L1 patterns are easily discernible. Yet the original hypothesis of CA that linguistic difference equals learning difficulty remains a definite oversimplification in the area of phonology. There are several other factors interacting with transfer that influence L2 pronunciation. The frequency of phonemes is one such factor. L1 phonological rules also interact with L2 phonological rules. Further, an early study by Nemser (1971) showed asymmetry of perception and production of L2 sounds. See also Broselow (1984), Corder (1983), Eckman (1981), McAllister *et al.* (2002); Wode (1980, 1986). Eckman (2004) is a comprehensive recent survey of phonological research in SLA.

A question frequently discussed in L2 phonological research is whether it is cross-linguistic similarity or cross-linguistic difference that causes more difficulties for the learner. The attempts at linguistic definitions of similarity and difference are, however, not necessarily based on the same criteria that learners use to perceive similarities and differences. The vagueness of perceived similarity with its individual variability in learners as well as the generally blurred relation between similarity and difference complicate matters for the researcher. As has been said before (p. 5), there must be an underlying similarity for meaningful differences to occur. This does not seem to have been sufficiently recognised. For phonology, it should also be remembered that only perception, not comprehension is involved, since phonological units do not have meaning. It is therefore probable that, as Corder has argued, the motor-perceptual skills of phonological reception and production behave differently from the organisational skills of planning and identification. Recognition processes as well as articulatory processes seem difficult to modify or extend.

> It may well be that the learning of motor-perceptual skills in language is indeed rather a process of classical conditioning than of discovery, and that imitation drill and pronunciation practice are consequently appropriate techniques for teaching them. Learning these skills in a new language may be more justly described as modifying or 're-shaping' existing behaviour than as acquiring a new set of rules. (Corder, 1973: 133)

When perception or production of pronunciation is tested there is generally also task rigidity involved: the learner's reactions or output must be fully native-like in order to be regarded as correct. If they are not native-like, they are regarded as erroneous. The sharp division between correct and incorrect does not square well with the blurred relation between similarity and difference. In general terms, Odlin (1989: 30f.) also criticises the oversimplified view based on error analysis that similarities of language are a greater source of difficulty than differences. He shows the improbability of the consequences of such a view. James (1980: 191) points out that sounds or structures of L2 that are non-existent in L1 'are not difficult once they have been identified to be learnt, but until they are, they will continue to be overlooked: this should not, however, be interpreted so much as their constituting a *learning* as a *recognition* difficulty.'

One special problem in pronunciation concerns such cognates as are formally similar (in writing often even identical) but are pronounced differently in L1 and L2. Even very advanced learners of related languages frequently go wrong in pronouncing such words. They produce the L1-pronunciation, even though they are proficient enough to be clearly aware of the general rules of L2-pronunciation that apply to these words. Apparently the L1-pronunciation is so deeply entrenched in the learner's mind that it resists modification, at least if the learner is tired or stressed. Advanced learners rarely make such mispronunciations of words that are very frequent in spoken language. Then the learner will have had many opportunities to hear and use the correct pronunciation, but proper names or infrequently-used similar words often belonging to a special vocabulary are frequently mispronounced by highly competent users of a non-native language.

Discourse and Rhetoric: Pragmatic Transfer

L2 discourse and L2 phonology are apparently similar in that L1 patterns in both of these are deeply entrenched in the learner's mind and thus are more resistant to modification and development than grammatical or, especially, lexical patterns. That discourse transfer has not been much investigated is no doubt partly due to the absence of explicitly stated norms for discourse, which makes the concept of error less applicable on units larger than the sentence. Also, investigating transfer in discourse, as well as the overlapping area of pragmatic transfer, requires the study of relatively advanced learners who already have sufficient linguistic resources in L2 at their disposal. Since in all linguistic areas reliance on L1 and languages other than the TL tends to be reduced as learning progresses, transfer-based constructions at the discourse level are not very common. Interesting comparisons between samples of L1 and L2 discourse have been made by, for example, Chafe (1980; see also Berman & Slobin, 1994; Connor, 1987), but these tend to be purely descriptive in nature, outlining differences between L1 and L2 use. They rarely provide an in-depth discussion of the underlying reasons for such differences. As is generally the case in comparative investigations, differences here also seem to be more interesting to researchers than similarities.

Odlin (1989: Ch. 4) is a succinct survey of work in the area up to the late 1980s. Research in discourse analysis presents a very diverse picture of the topics studied. In 1966, Kaplan had already suggested that language transfer of thought patterns may occur, that rhetorical organisational styles can be traced to L1. Still, manifestations of transfer are not very frequently documented in research. Kellerman (2001) is a small-scale study of Dutch learners of English where L1 in interaction with developing proficiency is found to influence narrative structure:

> The conclusion here is that there is transfer from Dutch, but it is transfer of the linguistic correlates of a developing narrative competence. The cognitive demands of the narration task seem to require a more linear,

less densely packaged style of narration from less experienced narra-tors. (Kellerman, 2001: 179)

Scarcella (1983) found that Spanish speakers introduced some conversa-tional L1-features into their L2 English, revealing a 'discourse accent'. In the same anthology, Bartelt (1983) studied transfer of L1 rhetorical processes, drawing his examples from the rhetorical redundancy of Apachean speakers writing L2 English. In a Finnish context, the high toler-ance threshold for silence combined with a low tolerance threshold for inter-ruptions may frustrate speakers from an Anglo-American or Mediterranean background – see Sajavaara & Lehtonen (1997), and below, pp. 110ff.

Tyler (1995) studied the miscommunication between a student, a native speaker of American English, and a tutor with Korean as his L1. The Korean's reliance on L1 conversational routines that were unexpected in an American context resulted in both participants viewing each other as non-cooperative. Linguistic causes are obviously not the only source of diver-gences between L1 and L2 discourse. Cultural and educational variations also have a very important part to play, and it is clear that linguistic transfer at discourse level interacts both with other types of transfer and with other language learning processes. We still know next to nothing about these interactions or about the positive aspects of discourse transfer. Also, the simple syntactic structures occurring in learner writing are paralleled in children's writing, and 'some discourse characteristics that appear to be due to native language influence may instead reflect little more than a normal development of writing abilities' (Odlin, 1989: 68)

Pragmatic transfer has come into the picture relatively late. An early, unusually thorough, MA thesis (Granbacka, 1985) showed that close cultural contact is more important than linguistic proximity in the restricted area of apologising. The Finnish and Finland-Swedish ways of apologising are very similar, but both differ from the English way. Trosborg (1987) also found that the use of modal markers in learner language differed from both native and target language norms.

Whether or not differences between native and non-native speakers are due to transfer is treated extensively by Nikula (1996). Nikula has assem-bled material from conversations both between native speakers of English and between native speakers of Finnish. She compares this with English conversations between native speakers and advanced Finnish non-native speakers. Her conclusion is that 'the greatest difference between the non-native and the native speakers (of English and Finnish alike) lies in the way they use implicit pragmatic force modifiers' (Nikula, 1996: 160) And 'the occasional bluntness in the non-native speakers' way of expressing their differing views is a sign of their insufficient mastery of modification strategies in the target language rather than a sign of native language influence' (Nikula, 1996: 136). Some evidence of (negative) pragmatic transfer can be found, but 'there is an obvious contrast between the learners' greater tendency to directness in the NS–NNS conversations and the abundance of pragmatic force modifiers in the Finnish conversations' (Nikula, 1996: 215). It is also difficult to find exact equivalences to pragmatic particles in another language, particularly as Finnish often uses clitics as pragmatic force modifiers, and direct item transfer of grammatical morphemes is rare (Odlin, 1989: 82, but see also Jarvis and Odlin, 2000, which shows indirect L1 influence in Finns' use of English prepositions).

Kasper and Rose (2002) is a comprehensive study of language learners' pragmatic development. Pragmatic transfer is not given much space here (basically, Kasper & Rose 2002: 153–157), and their discussion might be commented upon in the light of how I have seen transfer in other language areas.

Kasper and Rose begin their analysis outlining the correlation hypothesis, advanced by Takahashi and Beebe (1987), which predicts that second language proficiency is positively correlated with pragmatic transfer.

> Lower-proficiency learners ... are less likely to display pragmatic transfer in their L2 production than higher-proficiency learners because they do not have the necessary linguistic resources to do so. Higher-proficiency learners, on the other hand, do have such resources, so their L2 production will tend to reveal more pragmatic transfer. (Kasper & Rose, 2002: 153)

Kasper and Rose then describe a study by Maeshiba *et al.* (1996) that also deals with Japanese learners of English, which predicts that:

> transfer of apology strategies could be based on similarities and differences in assessment of contextual variables, with positive transfer occurring with similar assessments, and negative transfer where assessments differed. For the most part, these predictions were borne out. (Kasper & Rose, 2002: 154f.)

Kasper and Rose conclude that these results do not support the positive correlation hypothesis.

The apparent conflict between these studies might be resolved if we posit a basic threshold level of proficiency necessary for pragmatic transfer to appear in production. The learner needs to have both a fairly extensive vocabulary and some idea of how these words can be joined together. Once this stage has been reached, assumed similarities to L1 usage at the pragmatic level may come into play. However, as in other language areas, the effect of pragmatic transfer gradually weakens as proficiency develops. We know that pragmatic competence often lags behind linguistic competence and that even near-native speakers, who are generally able to avoid lexical and grammatical errors, frequently produce utterances which at least to some extent deviate from appropriate native usage and only in a few cases can be referred back to L1 influence (see the section on Non-native Proficiency in Chapter 10 below).

Pragmatic transfer in comprehension has to my knowledge not been much investigated. Also, what constitutes a pragmatic item is not at all clear. The problems of recognising positive transfer are heightened in pragmatics and in studies of psychotypologically close foreign languages: it is not easy to know exactly how L1-based sociopragmatic and pragmalinguistic knowledge is projected onto L2 contexts resulting in perceptions and behaviours not conforming to those of the target community. There is thus a great need for further studies of the processes behind pragmatic transfer investigating exactly what its part is in the development of sociolinguistic and pragmatic competence.

Grammar

As Odlin points out (1989: 68), children's L1 writing and adult learner language are often similar in that they both rely on very similar simple syntactic structures. This relates to the question of what type of grammar learners start out from. When does learning to produce a non-native language actually start? Learners do not start out from their L1 grammar, they start out from something much less complicated. It seems that the main adult language learning strategy is to reduce the target language to as simple a system as possible. R. Ellis suggests that the starting point consists of the early vocabulary that the learner has acquired.

> This is used in non-grammatical utterances, and conveys the learner's meaning with the help of information supplied to the listener by the context of situation. In other words, the starting point is the learner's knowledge of how to get a message across without the help of grammar. (Ellis, 1985: 70)

During the development of target-language competence a basic, simple grammar is achieved. This basic grammar is elaborated in response to the learner's exposure to the data of the target language, his previous knowledge of L1 and other languages, and his communicative needs (cf. Corder, 1979: 33, 1983: 90f.). Pienemann (1998: 73) states that, while even beginning second learners can make recourse to the same *general* cognitive resources as mature native language users, they have to create language-specific processing procedures. Transfer plays an important part in this elaborative process, but the details of this development, for example how transfer interacts with other processes, are still not clear. Possible universals in developing the L2 initial state seem to be too general or too abstract (cf. Rogers, 1997) to clarify the process on their own for the learner. For views advocating the importance of Universal Grammar (UG), see, for example, Eubank and Schwarz (1996). See also Eckman (1996), who convincingly argues that SLA can be explained without involving UG.

Learning L2 grammar 'involves abstracting regularities from the stock of known lexical sequences' (N. Ellis, 1997: 126). Similar regularities may or may not occur in the L1 or some other known language. The extent of congruence between grammatical categories is of special importance. When the L1 and L2 grammatical categories are largely congruent, the comprehension of lexical items (morphemes or words) is facilitated and the learner can approach the comprehension task without having to worry much about their syntactic relations. At an early stage of learning, high-frequency L2 function words, which are fundamental for comprehension to occur, are fairly easily identified with rough L1 equivalents. Where, on the other hand, the TL employs a different organisation of categories than the learner is used to from L1, comprehension and learning will be slower and the learner has to expend effort on learning to understand the under-lying system. Examples involving Finnish learners are English articles and prepositions, which are categories these learners are not used to in their L1. Swedish learners have a frame of reference that leads them to expect arti-cles and prepositions in a new target language. In Finnish, however, the relationships expressed by prepositions in Germanic languages are repre-sented differently. In Finnish most of them are not syntactic, but are morphophonemic in that they are normally expressed by case endings, not pre- or postpositions. The choice of correct prepositions certainly poses problems for any foreign learner of English but before Finnish learners can tackle such choice problems they have to solve the organisational problem of learning the functions of prepositions and establishing appropriate rough equivalences between prepositions in the TL and case endings in their L1.[1] Though there are correspondences between some Finnish case endings and some English prepositions, they are not in one-to-one relation-ships, which means that simple item learning does not work. While learners of related languages can establish simplified one-to-one corre-spondences of prepositions across languages with relative ease, Finnish learners meet with problems, as many Finnish case endings have a wealth of other functions apart from those of prepositions in Germanic languages. Learning how to use the underlying system of prepositions takes considerable time, because Finnish learners first have to learn to understand the function of prepositions (see also Jarvis & Odlin, 2000). For production they have to create a new category: they have to decide not only what preposition to use, but also whether a preposition should be used at all.

An important consequence of these difficulties is that, especially at early stages of learning, Finns tend to omit English prepositions and articles. These are not only difficult to learn, they are also difficult to spot for learners who do not have them in their L1. It is, for example, difficult for a Finn to understand why word order does not determine the choice of species in English, as it does in Finnish. *Talon edessä on auto* means 'there is a car in front of the house' while *auto on talon edessä* corresponds to 'the car is in front of the house'. Articles are certainly a problem areas for Finns, and no fewer than 85% of the article errors of Finnish 12-year-olds who had had three years of English at school were omissions (Herranen, 1978). Sajavaara (1983: 78) states that 'for some time at the beginning of English studies the mere existence of the category of the article is a problem for the learner.' Omission of articles because of influence from L1 Finnish can also be seen in subjects other than learners at school. A recent study (Rohlich, 2004) analysed miscues in reading aloud by informants representing three generations of Finnish immigrants to Australia. Articles were omitted very frequently by first-generation immigrants, though hardly at all by second-generation or third-generation immigrants in whom Finnish influence was now hardly noticeable. For immigrants, learning in a natural context probably also means that less attention will be paid to function words such as articles. Immigrants tend to be more concerned about communicative success than about linguistic accuracy. Articles affect communication only marginally and can therefore easily remain unnoticed at early and intermediate stages of learning. At early learning stages the underlying subconscious thinking seems to be that the category of articles is redundant (cf. George, 1972), i.e. not relevant since articles do not occur in L1. Other research, such as that of Oller and Redding (1971), has also shown that learners with articles in their L1 perform better on articles than learners whose L1 has no articles (cf. Duskova, 1969).

Omissions due to different linguistic structuring in the L1 and the TL have been found to occur in other areas and in other languages as well. Ryan's study (1997) shows the difficulty that Arab learners have with English vowels, owing to the secondary importance that vowels have in Arabic morphology, compared to consonants. When searching for an English word form, Arab learners not only substitute English vowels for each other, they often omit or misplace them, while the consonant structure of the English word is preserved. It appears that Arab learners, particularly at low level, tend to ignore the importance of English vowels and make 'an almost indiscriminate choice as to which vowel to use when one is needed' (Ryan, 1997: 189).

Ryan and also Schmitt and McCarthy, the editors of the volume in which Ryan's paper appears, rightly emphasise the importance of mastery of word forms for reading. Achieving such mastery will be delayed if cross-linguistic similarities in word forms cannot be easily established.

Language learning is primarily driven by the lexicon, but both grammar and lexis are important for the lexical item learning stage. 'Receptive knowledge of a word ... involves having an expectation of what grammatical pattern the word will occur in' (Nation, 1990: 31f.). In a natural learning situation, cross-linguistic identification of grammatical categories facilitates the establishment of one-to-one equivalences of individual items, while absence of transparent categories delays learning. The context of learning is relevant here: if lexical items are encountered only in isolation, syntactic relationships are irrelevant, and formal similarities, whether interlinguistic or intralinguistic, increase in importance. When new lexical items are encountered, their anchoring in memory is aided by prior knowledge of other, similar items stored near by (see also the earlier section on the mental lexicon, pp. 26ff.).

Some work relating to transfer has been generally sceptical about the existence of morphological transfer. However, as the recent paper by Jarvis and Odlin (2000) shows, transfer of bound morphology is also possible. This happens in a less direct way, in that, for example, the ways in which spatial information is organised in the L1 influences the way such information is realised in learner language. Bound forms are less isolable and perceptible than free forms and are rarely taken over directly. But the underlying L1 procedures are transferred: a primary counterpart of a case ending can in many cases be perceived. There is no formal similarity between an English preposition and a Finnish case ending, but there is procedural transfer that focuses on assumed oversimplified equivalences between the functions of English prepositions and Finnish case endings.

Where the grammatical categories exist in both the TL and the L1, the learner's task is easier. Errors in the choice of different English prepositions by Swedish-speaking learners largely reflect L1 usage (see also Granfors & Palmberg, 1976; Jarvis & Odlin, 2000). Learners' choices of some English prepositions differ depending on the way spatial information is coded in the learner's L1. Though Swedish prepositional usage in many respects differs from English, there is not a great deal of variation in the prepositional errors that Swedes make: in most cases they are clearly L1-based. Finns have much greater difficulties in establishing one-to-one correspondences between Finnish case endings and English prepositions, and the suggested erroneous prepositions (especially for multifunctional prepositions such as *of, on* and *by*) show a great variety. Finnish learners of English at early and intermediate stages commit more prepositional errors than Swedes, and a frequency study has shown that this is particularly true for Finnish learners at a lower proficiency level, who use fewer prepositions than do either Swedish learners at that level or native speakers (see Ringbom, 1987: 97ff.).

Lexis

Lexis was for a long time neglected in both linguistic and applied linguistic research, but this is certainly no longer the case. During the last two decades, at least, the fundamental importance of lexis has been recognised in SLA studies, and research on L2 vocabulary has expanded enormously (see especially the important work done by Meara, Singleton, Laufer and Nation and also several anthologies, notably the one by Schmitt and McCarthy, 1997).

Kellerman (1995: 137) makes the important point that cross-linguistic differences between languages predispose their speakers to conceptualise experience in different ways. Native speakers have learnt a conceptual-linguistic system for their L1. It is natural to try to make use of these underlying organisational principles of language when learning other languages, especially at the early stages.

L1 influence is consistently present in L2 lexical use. L2 learners have already learnt how their world and culture is reflected through language but they need new labels to relate the new language to prior knowledge. It is natural for learners to ascribe L1-based semantic properties and conceptual content to L2 words: they are reluctant to modify their conceptual L1-based system when learning another language. Pavlenko and Jarvis (2002) develop this thinking further in their discussions of conceptual and semantic transfer.

Lexical transfer in comprehension and production

When faced with the task of comprehending a new language, learners at early stages tend to employ lexical item transfer where possible. They try to associate new words with *primary counterparts* (Arabski's, 1979 term) in the L1. The search for primary counterparts is facilitated by formal cross-linguistic similarity of items: if such similarity can be perceived, item transfer is likely. Many words in a related language are easily guessable, at least as far as approximate meanings are concerned. Where there is semantic equivalence, which to a large extent depends on underlying cultural correspondences, primary counterparts are also more easily found. If there is both formal item similarity and semantic (near-)equivalence, receptive item learning will not require much effort.

Prototypicality is a key concept here: very often 'languages may have exact translation equivalents for words when they are used in their central senses, but not when they are used in more marginal or metaphorical ways' (Swan, 1997: 158). Jarvis (1997: 344) makes the same point: 'Learners' assumptions concerning which L1 and L2 words are translation equivalents are generally based on which L1 and L2 words have the closest central meanings, regardless of their peripheral meanings and semantic ranges'. Core meanings are more frequent and easier to learn than peripheral meanings. Item transfer in receptive learning means that the learner has made use of perceived formal and semantic similarities to connect a new item to prior linguistic knowledge in long term memory. It is true that, as for instance Singleton (1999) points out, much more is involved in learning words than connecting them with equivalent or partly equivalent L1-words. As their proficiency develops, learners realise that many words do not have a consistent one-to-one relation to words in another language. They will encounter polysemy and homonymy and understand that the same word may have different meanings in different contexts of occurrence. Inevitable adjustments of oversimplified equivalence relations, however, come at a later stage, as does understanding the various dimensions involved in knowing a word.[2] This is already system learning, not item learning. But establishing one-to-one connections is item learning, an essential first stage, and facilitation of learning very much depends on how natural it is to establish such relationships to prior knowledge. Across closely related languages this is a natural process, because of the many cross-linguistic similarities that can be perceived. Congruence in grammatical structure, grammatical system similarity, provides a good basis for facilitating lexical equivalences to be made.

In production, learners tend to stick to 'lexical teddy bears' (Hasselgren, 1994), i.e. words they feel safe with. They have established primary counterparts, which are generally overused. Immigrants with a limited amount of background education who have mainly learned the new language in natural situations often have a very restricted vocabulary (Kotsinas, 1983). Some immigrants to Sweden thus use the Swedish verb *fråga* ('ask') to refer to practically all words within the semantic field of verbal communication ('tell', 'discuss', 'say', 'explain', 'talk', etc.). In their interlanguage, the TL word takes on a wider meaning.

In advanced learners, preference for primary counterparts may result not necessarily in errors, but in stylistic infelicity and avoidance of more appropriate words (cf. K. Sjöholm, 1995). For advanced learners, educational and cultural background features seem to play roles at least as important as cross-linguistic correspondences between lexical items. Another source of errors made by advanced learners is what Laufer (1988, 1997) calls synforms, words with intralingual similarity.[3] General overviews of lexical transfer are given by Swan (1985, 1997).

Cognates

Related languages, and to a minor extent also unrelated languages because of possible loanwords, share a number of cognates.[4] Cognates in two languages can be defined as historically related, formally similar words, whose meanings may be identical, similar, partly different or, occasionally, even wholly different. Words with different meanings where the formal similarity is purely accidental, as in English *pain* – French *pain*, cannot be considered cognates. Technical and scientific terminology across Western and many other languages provides a large number of international words with only one meaning, which is generally transparent across Western languages. The transparency of such low-frequency special items means that learning these cognates presents little difficulty, especially since the Latin or Greek origin makes the terms similar in form practically everywhere. Finnish, however, does not include anything like as many of these loanwords as Swedish does. They are not of major interest for researchers, and will not be dealt with here.

It is easy for learners to get the meaning of cognates and in production they may be overused even by advanced learners in situations where a non-cognate would have been more appropriate. High-frequency words in one language may have low-frequency cognates in a related language. French learners thus tend to overuse 'commence' in spoken English, rather than the more frequent and appropriate 'start' or 'begin' (cf. Meara, 1993: 284f.).[5] Thus an important aspect of learning to master cognates actively is learning how their frequency and stylistic registers differ from the corresponding L1 words, since complete identification of meaning and function on the basis of similarity of form may lead to inappropriate use. For comprehension, however, French–English as well as Swedish–English cognates are undoubtedly facilitative.

An example of a special high-frequency cognate posing difficulties for intermediate learners is the word *fast*, which occurs in both English and

Swedish. Of the two different meanings in English, 'quick(ly)', 'rapid(ly)' and 'firm', 'stuck', as in *stand fast,* only the second, less frequently used type corresponds to Swedish. The Swedish word also has two different meanings. The adjective/adverb *fast* means 'firm', 'stuck', occurring for instance in the phrasal verb *åka fast,* 'be caught', literally 'drive stuck'. It is also a conjunction, 'although'. In a Matriculation Examination in non-native Swedish in Finland some years ago one topic for a composition was *'rattfylleristen åker fast',* meaning 'drunken drivers will be caught'. Most school leavers in Finnish-language schools knew English better than Swedish, and a sizeable proportion (probably more than 1%) of the several thousand candidates wrote their essays on the topic 'drunken drivers drive fast'.

A point worth emphasising is that this confusion between partly-deceptive cognates takes place across two non-native languages. Candidates from Swedish-language schools did not write on this topic, but if it had been given, hardly anyone would have misinterpreted the title. L1 knowledge of frequent words is firmly entrenched in the mind and is not as easily affected in comprehension by L2 knowledge as another non-native language is. Misunderstanding of a formally similar, but semantically partly deceptive, cognate can certainly occur in L2 comprehension, but the formal similarity will affect L2 production much more easily. It is then often manifested as complete language shifts. Beginning and intermediate learners make errors with high-frequency words, whereas more advanced learners tend to shift only formally similar words with relatively low frequency. Examples from Swedish candidates' Matriculation Exam scripts are *marmor* for 'marble' and *eremit* for 'hermit' (Ringbom, 1987: 146).

The misinterpretation of *åka fast* showed the influence of formal similarity from one non-native language to another related non-native language. However, accidental formal similarities even to an unrelated L1 may occasionally cause errors in foreign-language comprehension, at least if the context does not immediately rule out an interpretation as entirely implausible. One example of this comes from the reading comprehension part of the Matriculation Examination in English in 2003, in which an English text dealing with rare birds on a remote island said that black rats had destroyed almost the whole population. Not just one but well over half a dozen of the thousand scripts from Finnish-language schools that I read confused rats with *rastas,* the Finnish word for 'thrush', and the black thrush was thus undeservedly accused of having predatory qualities!

Form similarity to L1 as such does not ensure easy learning of the new word. The relative ease results from identity or close similarity in both form and meaning ... and from similarity in the derivation of the words in the two languages. (Laufer, 1990: 577).

While many cognates in the L1 provide useful pegs on which the learner can hang new L2-words, there are also deceptive cognates, 'false friends', which have a purely formal, but little or no semantic similarity. A recurring question for researchers and teachers is whether and to what extent cognates aid or hinder learning. In other words, are the good cognates more important for the learner than the false friends? There now seems to be general agreement on this question.

Vocabulary appears to be the area of which learners are most conscious and use of false friends often produces ludicrous or otherwise memorable effects in learner language. This means that deceptive cognates easily assume an importance in learners' and teachers' minds that is out of proportion to their significance. The dangers of deceptive cognates, however, should not be exaggerated, since the good cognates easily outnumber the deceptive ones. In fact, the ratio of good cognates to deceptive ones in English and French has been found to be approximately 11 to 1 (Hammer & Monod, 1976). Though this figure is probably an overestimation (Granger, 1993), the basic importance of positive transfer in lexis, as manifested especially in comprehension but also in production of cognates, cannot be doubted. Cognates classed as deceptive need not have totally different meanings: the meanings often overlap in that some senses of the TL word correspond to the cognate L1 word, while others do not. The resemblances between English and French vocabulary lie behind the result that French learners of English manage quite well with relatively infrequent Romance loanwords in a vocabulary test, but not very well with Germanic words, even though these are of higher frequency (Meara, n.d.).

Without guidance, however, there are many learners who will not make much use of cognates. Special training in recognising and forming cognates has therefore been advocated in some studies (Banta, 1981; Hammer & Giauque, 1989). On the basis of current research L2 speakers seem to be more reluctant to use cognates than one might expect them to be (see Meara, 1993; Lightbown & Libben, 1984). Teachers of a cognate language have to strike a balance in what and how much information on cognates they provide. The stage of learning is one relevant variable. At early stages, overemphasis on cross-linguistic similarities as they are manifested in cognates will facilitate the learning task, while more advanced learners, who have already developed their own individual learning strategies, may profit from at least some supplementary information on deceptive cognates and on the differences in register and frequency in the use of cognates.

The difference between meanings in some English and French cognates has for some words also spilled over into other languages, which have taken over the word from French and in its French sense, not the English one. French and Swedish thus share some English deceptive cognates such as *actual* (French *actuelle*, Swedish *aktuell*) and *fabric* (French *fabrique*, Swedish *fabrik*). Some other words that provide minor problems are those where there is a frequency difference. *Analphabet* is a very rare word in English, but corresponding to the noun *illiterate* in English are, for example, Swedish and Serbo-Croat *analfabet*.

The frequency of cognates naturally affects learning in that it is intimately connected with proficiency and stage of learning. High-frequency deceptive cognates are easily confused at early stages of learning. Initially, Swedish and German learners of English frequently confuse English *also* with Swedish *alltså* and German *also*, but since it is a high-frequency word this is generally a passing stage. The more the learner progresses in learning, the more input of the correct meaning of the word the learner gets, and this leads to a diminishing number of errors.

The difference between comprehension and production is particularly relevant to the role of cognates. For L2-comprehension, the context provides a set of cues for inferencing the meaning of an unknown word that do not exist for L2-production. Instances where the meanings of formally similar items are wholly different (they may be original cognates or merely similar by chance) are relatively few between English and Swedish. Wrong interpretation of deceptive cognates like this that have totally different meanings can often be prevented because the similar L1-word does not fit the context. There are, however, deceptive cognates where the context provides relatively little help for the learner. The most dangerous false friends for learners are those that occur in much the same context.[6] Such words are relatively rare, but when they are encountered in a text, even very advanced learners may misinterpret them. A particularly deceptive example from English–Swedish is the adjective *phoney*. The Swedish similar word is *fånig*, which also has a negative sense and occurs in similar contexts to *phoney*, but actually means 'silly' or 'ridiculous'. Highly competent Swedish learners, who have learnt to recognise the English word and rightly assume that it refers to something negative, may believe for a long time that it denotes something silly, rather than something false.

In contrast to the situation of L2 comprehension, L2 production provides no facilitative context that eliminates erroneous formally-similar words. An L2 word that is formally similar to an L1 word may be easily activated, even if its meaning is quite different from the intended one. Deceptive cognates cause many more errors in production than in comprehension.

It is natural that cross-linguistic similarities have mostly been discussed in the context of typologically related languages. However, even totally unrelated languages with little or no structural cross-linguistic similarity may exhibit surprising similarities, especially in lexis. This is above all manifested in the existence of loanwords, even high-frequency words. Harley referring to Yu, makes the point that:

> Even in languages that are typologically distinct, there may be specific lexical similarities that provide an advantage to the L2 learner. Thus a similarity in the lexicalisation of motion verbs in Chinese and English appears to give Chinese learners of English an advantage over Japanese learners in acquiring English motion verbs. (Harley, 1995: 9; see also Yu, 1996)

Another example that has received recent attention is the relation between Japanese and English. The Japanese lexicon of loanwords includes a large proportion of the high-frequency words in English. These loanwords, however, have been considerably modified and the similarities have been obscured particularly by the differences in scripts and phonological systems. This has led some teachers in Japan to believe that loanwords from English are a hindrance rather than a help: that they actually confuse learners and lead to unnecessary errors. Recent, more credible views, however, are that this built-in lexicon, *gairaigo,* provides a powerful tool for more effective learning that learners should make use of (Daulton, 2004; Uchida & Scholfield, 2000). Developing strategies for maximally efficient use of high-frequency English loanwords is a challenge for teachers and researchers in Japan.[7]

Language teachers have long recognised the importance of cognates, and there are several studies of the possible role of cognates, 'potential vocabulary', across Western European languages. They include Banta, 1981 (English and German); Denninghaus, 1976; Hammer and Monod, 1978, Pons-Ridler, 1984 (English and French) and Lübke, 1984 (German and French). Still, exploiting the similarities in teaching had not been 'systematically developed by course writers' (Meara, 1993: 282) until the appearance a few years ago of the EuroCom works (see below, pp. 103f.).

To establish the relative usefulness or hindrance of cognates to learning, and apply this to teaching procedures, the researcher needs to find out the importance and the interaction of at least the following variables given by Granger:

> (1) the degree of formal and semantic similarity, (2) to what extent cognates occur in similar contexts, (3) how frequent they are, and

whether they are core, non-core or subject-core items, (4) the learner's stage of learning, (5) whether the targeted L2-vocabulary is general or specialised and (6) whether they are encountered in comprehension or used in production. (Granger, 1993: 51)

These variables are also relevant to an assessment of the effect of chance similarities between words. Advanced learners of a related language hardly notice such chance similarities when they encounter formally similar but semantically wholly different words in a text. Even though *hug* is formally similar to Swedish *hugga* 'to chop (wood)', they are semantically wholly different, and occur in different contexts. Since the target language word does not belong to the most basic vocabulary in the language, learners are not very likely to encounter it during the early stages of learning. As for production, occasional errors might, however, occur even in the intermediate stages of learning.

For the learning of unrelated languages, learners do not generally expect to find formal similarities. If lexical chance similarities occur, the words tend to have very different meanings and occur in very different contexts. Thus Finnish *home* means 'mould' and *into* means 'eagerness', and the English words, though frequent, will hardly pose significant learning problem for Finns. From their L1 Finns are also used to seeing homonyms of totally different words in inflected forms. For example Finnish *muuta* can be either the partitive form of *muu,* 'other' or the imperative form of *muuttaa,* 'to move'. Most Finnish learners probably do not react to chance similarities between Finnish and English words, except possibly in the very early stages of learning.

Non-native Transfer

Transfer, most conspicuously in the area of lexis, occurs not only from the L1, but also from other languages known to the learner. If L2 and L3 are related, but L1 and L3 are not, it is natural for learners to look for whatever lexical and structural similarities they can perceive between L2 and L3. In an African or Asian context, a number of studies have found that previous knowledge of French (or English) influences the learning of English (or French) more than the learner's L1 does (see e.g Ahukanna *et al.,* 1981; Bentahila, 1975; Chumbow, 1981; Sikogukira, 1993; Singh & Carroll, 1979; Ulijn *et al.,* 1981, and the survey of research in the area in Cenoz, 2001). Linguistic and cultural/pragmatic factors are both similar in French and English, if they are compared with the differences between European and Asian/African languages. Within Europe, too, Lasagabaster (2000) found L2 Spanish to influence the learning of English more than L1 Basque did.

Within a wholly Indo-European context, more closely related L2-languages have also been found to influence L3 more than a less closely related L1 (Cenoz, 2001; Clyne, 1997, Clyne & Cassia, 1999; De Angelis, 2001, 2005; Dewaele, 1998; Hammarberg, 2001). But even totally unrelated non-native languages may provide support in the form of positive transfer, as indicated by the remark of a Finland-Swedish professor of sociology who had learnt Swahili during his two years as visiting professor in Tanzania. When asked whether it was difficult to learn Swahili, he replied: 'If you know Finnish (as L2) there will be no major problem learning Swahili' (see also Appendix 2). Such a statement may seem quite surprising, but these two languages do share some important characteristics. Above all, they are highly agglutinative. This means that in both languages words have a similar status as linguistic units; this is a pattern quite different from that existing in the Germanic languages, which the academic knew well as L1, L3, L4 and L5.

That knowledge of Finnish may facilitate the learning of Swahili illustrates the importance of perceived structural similarities across non-native languages. Facilitation due to chance similarities in morphemic structure between Finnish and Swahili seems even more likely if the learner has considerable L2-proficiency in one of the languages with a thorough declarative knowledge of its structure. Extensive declarative L2-knowledge may be more useful than L1-proficiency since it may be easier to understand and to verbalise what lies behind the concept, word or construction. The learner will not be exclusively confined to his native, more or less subconscious, feeling for the L1, important though it is, in understanding connections between the words.

Studies of non-native transfer in grammar are, however, sparse, and the few existing studies have focused mainly on errors. Some concrete evidence of non-native transfer on L3-learning has been found in grammar when conditions are conducive to transfer. This is the case, for instance, when there is extensive L2-input and the learner has a relatively high L2 proficiency (Stedje, 1977). Hammarberg and Williams' longitudinal studies of one L3 learner provide illuminating material here (Hammarberg, 2001; Williams & Hammarberg, 1998). They found that even the pronunciation of the L3 can be affected by an L2 if the L2 proficiency is high and the language is fresh in the mind. Recency is thus also a factor. There may also be a so-called 'foreign language effect': when they produce L3 words many learners seem to rely on lexical influence from a non-native language rather than from their L1, perhaps because of a subconscious fear of relying on their L1 (see Cenoz, 2001; Clyne, 1997; Clyne & Cassia, 1999; DeAngelis, 2001, 2005; Hammarberg, 2001). There is evidence that this can happen even when the non-native language is quite distant both from the target language and from the L1. Schmidt and Frota (1986) note cases of Arabic rather than L1 English lexical influence on L3 Portuguese. Selinker and Baumgartner-Cohen (1995) note lexical intrusions from both Hebrew and French in the learning of German. Also, Finland-Swedish learners who are fluent in Finnish may occasionally insert Finnish words in their English, at least at early stages of learning.

The many variables interacting with transfer are relevant also for L2 transfer on L3. Individual variations such as aptitude, personality, age, literacy, metalinguistic awareness, use of strategies, knowledge of the world and social background influence the amount of transfer in various ways. In addition to the differentiated role of transfer in comprehension, when compared with production, other relevant factors to consider are, for example, language prestige, mode of learning, order of acquisition and social context. It is easy to understand that a truly comprehensive view of transfer, where all of these, and a few others as well, are taken into account has so far not been possible. In the words of Odlin and Jarvis:

> Research has indicated that all of the following factors interact with cross-linguistic influence in the acquisition of languages beyond the second: language distance, source language proficiency, target language proficiency, order of acquisition of the languages, activation of source languages, formality of context, and constraints on verbal memory. (Odlin & Jarvis, 2004: 124)

Odlin (1989: Ch. 8, 2003; Odlin & Jarvis, 2004), as well as De Angelis (2001) provide good discussions of many of these issues.

While instances of non-native transfer may sometimes occur in both grammar and pronunciation, lexis is clearly the area where it is most obvious. Many multilinguals have had the experience that when they try to speak one foreign language, if it is one which they do not yet know very well, words from another language tend to intrude. The title of Selinker and Baumgartner-Cohen's paper (1995) is illustrative: 'Multiple language acquisition: "Damn it, why can't I keep these two languages apart?"'.

Lexical L2 transfer on L3 is, however, manifested somewhat differently from L1 transfer: there is a different distribution of errors due to item transfer and errors due to procedural transfer. Lexical item transfer in production is manifested in three different forms: (1) language shifts, (2) hybrids, blends and relexifications, and (3) deceptive cognates.

Language shift means that an L2 word is taken over from L2 into L3 in unmodified form. In contrast to other instances of item transfer, these transferred words need not be formally similar to the intended word.

Language shifts are particularly frequent in function words, notably function words that have a clear one-to-one correspondence in meaning to the intended word. The examples below come from Matriculation Examination essays written by candidates from Finnish-language schools (collected by Ringbom, 1987):

- Most fathers don't stay at home *fast* mother would like to go to work (Swedish *fast* = 'although').
- Men at the moment I have flu (Swedish *men* = 'but').
- Every person has bad *och* good sides (Swedish *och* = 'and').

These relatively rare errors were generally made by very weak candidates in the exam. In the Matriculation Examination of recent years there has been a marked decrease in their numbers, which is indicative of the general rise of standards in English in Finland. If complete language shifts are made by Finnish learners at this level, they tend to be more frequent from L2 Swedish than from L1 Finnish. Language shifts from Finnish are extremely rare in both Finnish candidates and Swedish candidates in the Matriculation Exam.[8] Where there is reliance on L1 Swedish in the form of language shifts it tends to occur only in low-frequency translation equivalents similar in form to the intended English word (*marmor* and *eremit).*

Learners who are not very advanced may occasionally insert semantically equivalent words from another non-native language. This seems to happen when attention slackens, since what are transferred are primarily function words and other items not really essential to communicative efficiency. The most frequent examples of completely shifted non-native words in the English of Finnish Matriculation Exam scripts are Swedish *men* 'but', *och* 'and' and *fast* 'although', as quoted above (Ringbom, 1987: 147ff.). These words, though formally by no means similar to the intended words, are functionally and semantically equivalent to the corresponding English items. They are used as links between more salient elements in the text and such links appear to get less close attention by the speaker/writer, which results in a slip into the wrong non-native language (cf. DeAngelis, 2005; Vildomec, 1963: 170). That two of these three most frequently shifted words also occur in English, though totally different in meaning, may also have contributed to their use.

There seem to be several factors contributing to the complete shift of units from a non-native language: one-to-one semantic relationship, formal similarity, early stage of learning, and unstressed function words. At least two of these are probably needed for language shifts to occur, but since there is considerable variation among learners in that some learners do not confuse languages whereas many others do so at least occasionally at early stages of L3 learning, the most important variable here will probably have to be sought in individual learner characteristics: how able the learner is to keep the languages apart.

Hybrids, blends and relexifications illustrate various forms of mixing of L2 and L3 units. In hybrids and blends, L2-forms may be taken over into L3 with some L3 modifications such as L3 nominal or verbal endings or changes in spelling:

- All these wooden *golves* must be cleaned (Swedish *golv,* singular and plural, = 'floor').
- I was much *pigger* after the walking out. (Swedish *pigg* = 'refreshed').

Relexification means that a word from another language is modified phonologically to fit in better with assumed TL norms. Thus Swedish L2-words have been relexified into a form perceived to be more 'English-like':

- In the morning I was tired, but in the evening I was *piggy.*
- I couldn't speak about *allthing* with them (Swedish *allting* = 'everything').
- I don't believe it's your *fale* that you have put the cheque in the wrong envelope (Swedish *fel* = 'fault').
- Now I must *slut*, but I hope you will write soon (Swedish *sluta* = 'finish').

Since Swedish and English are related languages, there are a number of deceptive cognates between the two. Finnish learners, just like Swedish learners, often go wrong with these words. Examples showing formal similarity coupled with semantic difference or only partial similarity between these pairs are:

- I have also *proved* few times smoking (Swedish *prova* = 'try').
- Men in Finland have taken *stocks* from forests (Swedish *stock* = 'log').
- The society would *spare* a lot of money (Swedish *spara* = 'save').
- There are lot of snow on *ways* and streets (Swedish *väg* usually = 'road' but sometimes also 'way').

These examples show item transfer from L2, and formal similarity L2 – L3 plays a crucial part for learners who are generally not very advanced. Swedish-speaking learners also fall into the trap of using deceptive cognates, which have formal similarity to their L1 but no, or only partial semantic correspondence. If we, on the other hand, look for errors due to formal similarities between English and Finnish, they will be very hard to find. There simply are very few direct lexical similarities between the languages. Some rare errors due to chance similarities between low-frequency words do, however, occur in the Matriculation Exam essays:

- Our *perils* will see what we have had and will understand us better (Finnish *perillinen* = 'descendant').

An example of untypical errors in comprehension due to formal similarity between English and Finnish is given above, p. 74.

The Matriculation Exam essays, however, also provide many examples of transfer not of items, but of lexical procedures. One category is calques, i.e. loan translations of multi-word units. L1-based errors like the following are often made in the essays:

- Horses are the most dignified *home animals* (Finnish *kotieläin* = 'domestic animal', literally 'home animal').
- Basketball, football and *flyingball* are popular (Finnish *lentopallo* = volleyball, literally 'flying ball').
- It was *raining snow* in June (Finnish *sataa lunta* = 'to snow', literally 'to rain snow').
- *Football company* (Finnish *jalkapalloseura* = 'football club', *seura* = both 'club' and 'company').

Arguably the most frequent type of transfer-induced errors in the essays is, however, extension of meaning on the basis of L1:

- To my family *heard* also father and mother (Finnish *kuulua* = 'be heard' and 'belong').
- He is the other of the two accepted *seekers* (Finnish *hakija* = 'applicant', from *hakea,* most commonly 'to seek').
- I *came* unhappy in the autumn (Finnish *tulla* most commonly = 'come', more seldom 'become').

This type of error is common in both Finnish and Swedish learners. Table 5 is compiled from the material in Ringbom (1987: Appendix) and shows the frequency of lexical item transfer from non-native Swedish in Finnish learners.

While Swedish learners make errors due to Swedish as a result of either item transfer or procedural transfer, the picture for the Finns is different.

Table 5 Lexical transfer errors due to non-native Swedish noticed in some 11,000 Matriculation Exam essays in English written by Finnish students

Complete language shift	197
Hybrids, blends and relexifications	75
Deceptive cognates	162

Finns do not make the same use of Swedish in their errors. What is striking is that the extensive material here does not show any non-native transfer occurring in Swedish-based loan translations or semantic extension. Some such cases would undoubtedly come to light in a thorough search, but they would be very few in number, and would probably have been made by candidates with a good knowledge of Swedish. Non-native lexical transfer tends to be item transfer, occurring either on the basis of formal similarities or, occasionally, as instances of language shift.

There are clearly problems with frequency tables based on material in essays, and only a rough idea of the frequency of different types of L2-based lexical errors in essays can be gained from Table 5. The frequencies of different types of transfer-induced lexical errors were, however, also investigated in a translation task, the results of which were originally published in Ringbom (1978) and again in Ringbom (1987). Here 577 students from Finnish-language schools and the same number from Swedish-language schools in Finland were asked to translate into English (their L3) 63 selected L1 words, given in otherwise English sentences. The subjects were 16–17-year olds from grammar schools (before the Finnish school system went comprehensive), who had read English for at least seven years at school, and who also knew Finnish and Swedish respectively as their L2. The difference between the test types of essays and a translation is relevant in that complete language shifts do not figure prominently in a test where only one word has to be translated. Table 6 shows the distribution of errors.

Table 6 Lexical transfer errors in translations

	Influence from			
	Finnish (L1)	*Swedish (L2)*	*Finnish (L2)*	*Swedish (L1)*
A Language switches	0	33	0	20
B Hybrids and blends	16	68	1	87
C Deceptive cognates	9	61	6	208
D Calques	404	2	14	199
E Semantic extensions	153	0	0	135
Total	*582*	*164*	*21*	*649*

Note: Finns (*n* = 577), Swedish-speaking Finns (*n* = 577)
Source: Ringbom (1987)

The same type of test was given by Dahlin (2001) to students at three Finnish and three Swedish schools in south-western Finland. Twenty-five words were tested, seven of which (*dozen, tongue, blush, matches, bachelor, jam* and *stamps*) also occurred in Ringbom's test. 440 subjects took part, 173 Finns, 151 Swedes and 116 bilinguals (87 of whom came from Swedish-language schools). Most of the subjects had studied English for seven years or more. One difference from the subjects in Ringbom's study was that the Finnish speakers had English as their L2 and Swedish as their L3. This is a partial explanation of a general improvement in the Finns' test results.

Figures compiled from Dahlin's material are shown in Table 7 (the bilingual students were not included). This shows the same trend as Table 6: procedural transfer as manifested in calques and semantic extension errors reflects L1 influence, very seldom influence from a non-native language.

Another example of the same trend can be seen in a recent MA thesis by Järviaho (2004). She gave an English cloze test, without giving the sought words in the L1, to Finnish and Swedish comprehensive school students in Kristiinankaupunki/Kristinestad, a Western Finnish town with closely similar proportions of Finnish and Swedish inhabitants.

From a research point of view, the disadvantage of vocabulary tests is that the words tested are chosen by the tester, not by the learners themselves. Largely, the proportions of item transfer and procedural transfer are determined by what kind of a word is tested: in words having cross-linguistic similarity there will be item transfer, while words showing

Table 7 Lexical transfer errors in translations into English made by Finnish and Swedish teenagers from upper secondary schools in South-western Finland

	Procedural transfer		*Item transfer*[10]
Influence from	*Calques*	*Semantic extensions*	*Deceptive cognates, hybrids, blends, language shifts*
Finns (n = 173)			
Finnish (L1)	32	21	47
Swedish (L2)	0	0	23
Swedes (n = 151)			
Finnish (L2)	9	0	2
Swedish (L1)	47	44	150

Based on Dahlin (2001)

procedural transfer typically are compounds, verbal phrases or poly-semous words. Supplementary material from free production showing the learner's rather than the tester's choice of words is therefore needed. The same picture, however, emerges from both types of tests.

The present foreign language situation in Finland, in which English has replaced Swedish as the general L2 and Swedish is mostly an L3, means that non-native influence of L2 English on the learning of L3 Swedish is now a frequent phenomenon. This can be confirmed by any teacher of Swedish in Finnish-language schools. Laitakari (2001) made a study of Swedish compositions written by Finnish comprehensive school students aged 15-16. In Table 8 we can again see the same pattern of the proportion of L1-based vs. L2-based lexical errors.

Table 8 shows that when the target language is a language other than English we find the same pattern: non-native lexical transfer is manifested differently from L1-transfer. Here, too, lexical errors due to non-native transfer are nearly always the outcome of item transfer normally based on an assumed cross-linguistic *formal* similarity (typically deceptive cognates, relexifications and blends).

On the other hand, in learners non-native procedural transfer, as exemplified by calques and instances of semantically wrongly extended words due to L2 influence, is conspicuous by its absence. The perceived distance between languages, as it is manifested in formal cross-linguistic similarities, as well as the status of native or non-native language are prime factors determining the extent and type of transfer.[9] When procedural transfer errors, as manifested in calques and semantic extensions, occur in either Finnish- or Swedish-speaking learners of English, they are quite consistently made on the basis of the learner's L1, not on another non-native language. For item transfer, on the other hand, perceived cross-linguistic similarity is an important prerequisite, occurring at all stages of learning.

Table 8 Lexical transfer errors in Swedish (L3) compositions made by Finnish comprehensive school students with English as their L2 ($n = 180$)

	Procedural transfer		Item transfer
Influence from	*Calques*	*Semantic extensions*	*Deceptive cognates, hybrids, blends, language shifts*
Finnish (L1)	63	51	9
English (L2)	5	2	130

Based on material in Laitakari (2001)

Procedural transfer requires native-like or very advanced proficiency in the language from which transfer takes place. Dagut (1977: 224) already made the point that the learner 'will intuitively transfer to the foreign language the lexical segmentation that *his own tongue* [my italics, HR] has accustomed him to finding normal and natural'.

L1 transfer is not alone in being treated as if it had purely negative consequences. We can also find references to, for example, how knowledge of English is regarded as being detrimental to the learning of German word order in schools in Sweden (Håkansson, 1994). This is a consequence of transfer having been studied almost exclusively in terms of errors. But overall, it can hardly be doubted that L2 transfer, too, has predominantly positive effects, above all for comprehension.

If we try to understand the consequences that knowledge of one non-native language may have for acquiring a productive competence in a related new language, it seems fair to assume that a high threshold level of proficiency has to be reached in L2 for genuine facilitation of L3 learning to occur. Otherwise assumed similarities primarily lead to errors in production. They do, however, help in comprehension.

Notes

1. The distinction between choice problems and organizational problems was made by Galanter (1966).
2. Discussions of what knowing a word means are, for instance, Laufer (1997); Nation (1990: 29ff.); Richards (1976); Ringbom (1987: 36ff.).
3. A taxonomy of intralingual similarities leading to learners' errors is given by Laufer (1997: 147f.). The most problematic types were those that differed according to suffixes (*industrial – industrious, comprehensible – comprehensive*) and synforms identical in consonants but different in vowels (*adopt – adapt, proceed – precede*).
4. Early papers dealing with English cognates, especially deceptive cognates, in relatively distant languages are e.g. Welna (1977) for Polish, Gociman and Bantas (1976) for Romanian, and Ivir (1968) for Serbo-Croat.
5. The overuse of at least some Romance words in English by French learners must be balanced against the general tendency in all learner language to overuse the most frequent Germanic verbs such as *take, put, find, think* and *get*. See Granger (1996); Ringbom (1998).
6. For a brief list of some particularly dangerous English–Swedish cognates, see Appendix 1.
7. There appear to be other cross-linguistic similarities as well that Japanese learners might make use of when learning to read English (see Brown & Haynes 1985; Koda, 1997). But even learners of languages more similar to European languages than Japanese need explicit guidance on how to take advantage of cognate relationships (cf. Harley *et al.*, 1986; Lightbown & Libben, 1984; Wesche & Paribakht, 1996).
8. L1 function words are probably more frequently switched into L2 in an oral

context, than in writing. Pietilä, who studied the speech of Finnish immigrants to the US, provides some examples (1989: 191f.) of L1 Finnish function words being switched into spoken L2 English, even though they had no phonetic resemblance to the corresponding English words.

9. An example of the strength of perceived similarity to a non-native language is also given by K. Sjöholm (1995), who compared advanced Finnish and Finland-Swedish learners' linguistic choices in a specially designed test in English. His test instrument comprised 28 multiple-choice items where two alternatives were fully acceptable in the context, one being a phrasal verb (*take off*) and the other a (near-) synonymous one-part verb (*remove*). Phrasal verbs hardly exist in Finnish, but they are frequent in Swedish. Native speakers of English consistently preferred the phrasal verbs in Sjöholm's test, while Swedish and especially Finnish learners tended to choose the one-part verb much more frequently. Seven of Sjöholm's phrasal verbs were transparent to Swedish speakers, i.e. of a type where Swedish makes use of the same construction as English. In contrast to the general trend in the test, where Swedish learners chose more phrasal verbs than the Finns, Sjöholm found that his Finnish learners chose these seven phrasal verbs more than the Swedes did. Based on perceived similarity as a contributing reason, he suggests non-native influence from Swedish.

10. The figure for L1 item transfer from Finnish in this table may seem surprisingly large. This is partly explained by the choice of the tested words being largely governed by the tester's attempt to select words with some formal similarity to either the Finnish or Swedish target word. The most frequent example of L1 item transfer from Finnish is *postmarks* for 'stamps' (Finnish *postimerkki*) (11 instances). Other examples are *jello(w)* for 'jam, jelly' (*jelly* + Finnish *hillo*, 'jam') (10 instances), *sticks* for 'matches' (Finnish (*tuli*)*tikkuja*) (4) and the replacing of the initial sound /t/ for /d/ in *tusin*, (3), *tosen(s)* (3) and *tusen* (2) for 'dozen' (Finnish *tusina*).

Chapter 9
Skill Theory, Automaticity and Foreign Language Learning

Already having mastered a related task when you have to perform a new one may be either a help or a hindrance. Word translation has been found to be fastest when the prompt word is a cognate of the target word (Lotto & de Groot, 1998). Yet some (early) investigations emphasise the inhibiting effect of a previously-mastered skill. Some reaction time studies have shown that there are consistently longer latencies for judgments where there are formally similar competing items. This is what psychologists call homogeneous inhibition, *'homogene hämmung'* (Juhasz, 1970: 93ff.). However, if this knowledge is applied to the relevance of transfer to language learning, it need not contradict the conclusions of numerous SLA studies that previous relevant knowledge facilitates, not hinders, the learning of a new, related language. We must take into consideration the nature of the task itself. If the task is rigidly defined and allows for little or no deviation from the expected pattern (such as performing a second Scottish dance immediately after you have learnt a first) the previously acquired skill easily causes confusion. In the area of language learning this is the situation for mastering spelling, where the notion of error is basic and can be specified as being a deviation from a clearly defined norm. Spelling is a highly specific task related to problem solving: there is normally only one correct solution and anything that is not fully correct must be regarded as wrong.[1] It is not surprising that learners with a Roman alphabet as their L1 apparently make more spelling errors than learners with a non-Roman L1-alphabet (Oller & Ziahosseiny, 1969). If, on the other hand, there is considerable flexibility in the task to be mastered, as is the case especially in language comprehension, learning the new task will be facilitated by the possession of a related skill. Learning to play a new ball game similar to one you already master allows for considerable flexibility and illustrates the facilitative effect of a previously-acquired related skill.[2] A tennis player finds it easy to keep the ball in play in squash, while the soccer player has greater problems with this.[3] Language learning taken as a whole, and comprehension in particular, leaves considerable room for deviations, because learners with an L1 related to the TL can make good use of their previous knowledge for attaining approximate comprehension. Learners with a zero or near-zero similarity relation to the TL, on the other hand, have to start the learning from a lower platform.

Differences in the nature of the task to be performed are so great that generalisations on the basis of a rigid task (i.e. any test type where there are no alternatives other than 'right' or 'wrong') are not easily applied to flexible tasks, or vice versa. A corollary to the relevance of task specificity would be that language teaching of a traditional grammar-translation type, with its strongly normative character allowing little deviation from what the teacher expects, reduces the advantages that learners of related target languages have compared with learners with an unrelated L1. This is in accordance with my impression of the differing results between the old and the new type of Matriculation Examination in Finland. The old exam type, which was compulsory up to 1976, optional from 1977 to 1979 and wholly absent from 1980 onwards, consisted entirely of translation from and into the target language. At a meeting lasting one whole day, 15–20 national examiners had to agree on how many points should be deducted for any real or predicted translation error, and the sum of minus points was then converted into a 5-degree scale of marks. The new exam in foreign languages, which came into effect in 1980 and has since undergone only minor changes, is more comprehensive, and comprises a listening comprehension part, a reading comprehension part and a written composition. The differences in performance in favour of the Swedish-language schools clearly seemed to increase when the new comprehensive exam type was introduced. When more communicative and more comprehensive test types are introduced, they seem to favour speakers of a related L1 more than when a typically accuracy-oriented test type such as translation has a monopoly.

Item and system similarities have an effect on the learner's procedural knowledge: automatised procedures used for comprehending and producing L1 can more naturally and easily be used for L2 when the target language is a language with many formal similarities to L1. That comprehension often works even if it is merely approximate means that there is more flexibility in a comprehension task than in a production task, where not only communicative success but also linguistic accuracy must be taken into consideration.

Making use of perceived similarities, both intralinguistic and cross-linguistic, is part of what learners learn to do as their proficiency develops. As procedural knowledge of the target language improves, there will be increasing automaticity in retrieving mechanisms. Fluency in reception and production is based on automatised processing. Rapid recognition of cognates relies on automatised procedures. L1 words are already fully automatised in long-term memory, and the automatised L1 procedures need to be only minimally changed for retrieving a word which is both phonologically and semantically similar.

Anderson's ACT* theory (outlined in Segalowitz, 2003; Singley & Anderson, 1989) is a further development and resurrection of Thorndike's classic work in psychology from the early years of the 20th century. According to Anderson, skill acquisition involves a transition from a stage characterised by declarative knowledge to one characterised by procedural knowledge. Skill acquisition requires a gradual automatisation of component subskills through practice. DeKeyser (2005) makes the point that proceduralisation, the transition from declarative to procedural knowledge, is the bottleneck in second language skill development. He emphasises the importance of explicit learning and systematic practice to remedy the situation. Automatisation of procedural knowledge requires a lot of practice and takes a long time.

As far as reading comprehension is concerned, however, the subskill of vocabulary knowledge can take the learner a long way. 'Automaticity of single word recognition underlies fluency (in reading)' (Segalowitz, 2003: 398). For listening comprehension and production, additional skills also have to be developed (see above, pp. 58ff.).

Developing automaticity in listening-comprehension procedures is extremely important. Poor listeners spend much processing time on individual items because they do not recognise them automatically. This means that there is not sufficient time for comprehension of the larger meaning of the message. Conference participants listening to papers in a language they do not know well are clearly aware what this means. But 'if one can handle the phonology and syntax of a second language automatically, then more attention can be paid to processing semantic, pragmatic, and socio-linguistic levels of communication' (Segalowitz, 2003: 400f.). Automaticity as evidenced in greater language proficiency reflects a qualitative change in the way that linguistic information is processed, not just in an increased speed in processing. The cross-linguistic similarities that exist between English and Swedish facilitate automatisation of items and procedures in Swedish learners of English.

The Use of Cross-linguistic Similarities at Different Stages of Learning

When do cross-linguistic similarities affect the learning process most? It is natural to assume that it especially affects the early stages of learning, when a limited competence in the TL means greater reliance on cross-linguistic relations while only few intra-lingual similarities can be perceived. 'Advanced learners are affected by cross-linguistic influence in different ways from beginners, but simply because they know more and their knowledge opens up new susceptible areas' (Kellerman, 1984: 121). Jessner (2003: 49) also makes the point that the learner develops skills and qualities that cannot be found in an inexperienced learner.

In comprehension, the picture is fairly clear: from the very beginning learners profit from similarities they perceive, especially formal similarities, which help them to establish cross-linguistic equivalences. Since many of these equivalences are oversimplified, they will be modified by subsequent system learning, and there will not be the same overwhelmingly positive effect of transfer at later stages of learning a related language. Still, the size of the learned receptive vocabulary is crucial for the quality of comprehension, and in this respect learners (especially if they learn a closely-related language) may reach a level exceeding that of many native speakers of a lower educational level. An extensive vocabulary is, however, less relevant for success in listening than it is in reading: compared even with advanced learners, native speakers have the advantage of having encountered much more input and a much wider variety of local dialects. These pose problems for most foreign learners, who tend to have experience of only one variety taught in the classroom, a standard language.

The learner's vocabulary develops both quantitatively ('breadth of knowledge', 'vocabulary size') and qualitatively ('depth of knowledge', 'vocabulary organisation') as learning progresses. Though measuring vocabulary size poses practical problems, mostly depending on the difficulty of determining what a word is, the quantitative aspects can at least in theory be described in simple terms: the learner gradually masters a larger number of items and structures both receptively and productively. The qualitative aspects are more complex, and reflect system learning rather than item learning (see also Haastrup & Henriksen, 2000; Laufer, 1991). The learner's progress in learning involves at least the following: (1) learning more about the different parameters of lexical knowledge (what it means to know a word) and modifying oversimplified one-to-one hypotheses of item learning; (2) transition from receptive to productive competence; (3) transition from dependence on form in storing the items to dependence on meaning when establishing a lexical network of links between L2 words in the mind. 'Lexical progression involves a process of network building where the organisational links in the mental lexicon are strengthened, e.g. through a process of gradual differentiation within a certain lexical field' (Haastrup & Henriksen, 2000: 222). Much more research is needed in these areas, but cross-linguistic lexical similarity clearly seems to be less important during the later stages than during the earlier stages of learning, since it affects item learning more than system learning. The development of learners' vocabulary is outlined by Henriksen (1999), who distinguishes between three separate but related vocabulary dimensions: (1) partial-precise knowledge; (2) depth of knowledge and (3) receptive-productive dimensions.

The psychotypological factors are crucial where L2 comprehension is concerned. When it comes to production, the picture is not so clear. In general terms, perceived cross-linguistic similarities leading to the establishment of at least approximate equivalences are no doubt useful for production, too – if not for other reasons, at least because it requires less effort to convert receptive knowledge into productive knowledge than to acquire productive knowledge from scratch. We must not forget the interaction that takes place between comprehension and production. Still, opinions differ as to the precise effects of cross-linguistic similarities in production. Thus Corder (1977: 11) stated that 'the second languages that we may be least likely to master satisfactorily are those which are either the closest to, or the most distant from, our mother tongue.' While there is nothing to disagree with in the view that learning the most distant languages requires the largest amount of work, the replacement of one word is necessary for the statement to hold true also of closely-related languages. Mastery of language in Corder's terms seems to denote truly native-like performance. If, and only if, the word 'satisfactorily' is replaced by 'perfectly' Corder's statement is probably true for closely-related languages. To climb the last step on the ladder of language learning and reach truly native-like speaking competence is a stage where cross-linguistic similarity either has no significance at all or may even have a predominantly negative effect. What distinguishes near-native proficiency from fully native-like competence depends primarily on the learner's ability and amount of practice, not very much on the linguistic distance between L1 and L2. But well over 90% of foreign language learners do not reach a near-native stage where they might even for a time be taken for natives. Ordinary learners of a language related to the L1 learn to communicate fairly successfully in a relatively short time thanks to the aid provided by perceived cross-linguistic similarities – see further the discussion in Ringbom (1987: 56f.), and also E. Ingram (1975: 273) and James (1991: 250ff.). As for Corder's statement about the problems of mastering closely related languages, the Scandinavian situation outlined above (pp. 12ff.) pinpoints the absence of a necessity to learn to produce a closely-related language perfectly, since communication generally works if everybody speaks the L1.

Bilingual vs. Monolingual Language Learners

One question that has occupied researchers for a long time is whether it is easier to learn a new language if you already know one non-native language.

Nearly all studies conclude that this is the case. The closer the non-native language is to the TL, the more it helps, as has been shown by the many studies of African or Asian learners referred to above (pp. 78ff.). There are, however, many constraints that need to be considered. Degree of proficiency, mode of learning, language prestige, input, individual variables, and order of acquisition are all relevant variables (see e.g Albert & Obler, 1978; Clyne *et al.*, 2004; Cummins, 1978; De Angelis, 2001: 67–74; Jessner, 1999; Marx & Hufeisen, 2004; McLaughlin & Nayak, 1989; Thomas, 1988,1992.) The psychotypological issue of whether the two non-native languages are similar or not is especially relevant, but there are cases where other variables have been found to be even more important.

In an MA thesis, Vesterlund and Till (1982) made a comparative study of Finland-Swedish learners of English at commercial colleges in the towns of Helsinki, Turku/Åbo, Mariehamn and Vaasa/Vasa. The subjects were divided into a bilingual Swedish/Finnish and a monolingual Swedish group.[4] The results were surprising in that the monolingual group performed better than the bilinguals. There is, however, a natural explanation for this. The bilingual population was recruited from the cities of Helsinki and Turku, university towns where commercial colleges are not very prestigious, and mainly attract students who do not have either the required merits or the inclination for university studies. Particularly the monolingually Swedish Åland town of Mariehamn, on the other hand, has comparatively few study alternatives after comprehensive school, and the local commercial college, at least in the 1980s, enjoyed quite high prestige and attracted many good students. This difference could also be seen in the fact that the monolinguals in the study achieved better school marks than the bilinguals both in English and generally.

Another MA thesis on the same topic by Ek and Tani a little later (1985) made necessary adjustments in their selection of subjects. Bilinguals and monolinguals were here taken from Swedish-language colleges in towns comparable in size and in educational opportunities (Ekenäs/Tammisaari, Jakobstad/Pietarsaari, Porvoo/Borgå and Mariehamn. The results were then what could be expected: the bilinguals performed better. A recent MA thesis by Järviaho (2004) investigated comprehensive school students in Kristiinankaupunki/Kristinestad, which is a town in Western Finland evenly matched for Finnish and Swedish. Järviaho also found that the bilinguals performed better than either the Swedish or the Finnish peer group. However, the different results in these studies clearly illustrate the danger of drawing generalising conclusions on the basis of only one variable: that of bilingualism/monolingualism.

Most of the studies referred to above seem to be in basic agreement about some general issues. Since bilinguals can draw on not one but two languages they have the advantage over monolinguals in many language-related skills. Bilinguals have a greater metalinguistic awareness and they can see the possibilities of expressing the same idea by different linguistic means. They are concretely aware that there is more than one way to communicate linguistic meaning. They are also more sensitive to the systematic nature of language. However, it seems that the level the bilingual has attained in both languages needs to be high for the learner to take real advantage of his/her other language (cf. De Bot, 2004: 22). Also, they may need to have parallels between L2 and L3 pointed out to them (see O'Laoire, 2004). Ideally, the learning situations of L2- and L3-learning should be as similar as possible for L2-knowledge to facilitate L3-learning. If the L2 has been learnt in a natural environment it may not help classroom learning of L3 as much as natural L3-learning and classroom learning of L2 may facilitate natural L3-learning less than natural L2-learning does (Thomas, 1988: 240).[5]

While there seems to be no doubt that a bilingual is helped by his/her knowledge of two languages, this seems to be more obvious at early stages of learning than later on. It is not at all clear whether bilinguals are more or less likely than monolinguals to reach native-like proficiency in a new foreign language. That is, however, a stage that only a minute minority of learners ever reach.

While psychotypology clearly is a main reason for the differences between Swedes and Finns in learning English, another reason no doubt plays an important part as well: the general Swedish/Finnish bilingualism of Swedish-speaking Finns. With the exception of the Åland Islands and a few other monolingually Swedish communities in Ostrobothnia on the west coast, Swedish speakers are surrounded by a massive amount of Finnish. At an early stage most children realise that they simply have to learn Finnish in order to get along in society, and even in communities which are predominantly Swedish-speaking the teaching of Finnish in Swedish-language schools generally leads to early learning of a basic fluency in speaking. For most Finnish speakers, on the other hand, Swedish is a language not much encountered outside the classroom except perhaps on a few TV programmes. When analysing the reasons for the differences between Finnish and Finland-Swedish learners of English, the better metalinguistic awareness found to be a characteristic of bilinguals clearly has some part to play, not only the psychotypological aspect of Swedish being perceived to be close to English. Early bilingualism of Swedish-speaking Finns may also partially explain why at school level they seem to perform at least marginally better than their peers in Scandinavia (see the section on international evaluations above, and pp. 108f. below). Bilingual learners may find it easier than monolinguals to develop useful learning and communication strategies.

Notes

1. Oller (1972) discussed transfer, mainly in L1 acquisition. Like behaviourists, he rightly focused on degrees of similarity, not similarity vs. difference. For interference, negative transfer, he stated the following conditions (1972: 29): '(1) the items to be stored or retrieved must be functionally identical on some but not all of the cognitive dimensions utilized for storage. (2) They must be in or near the focus of attention at nearly the same time.' According to Oller, increasing similarity would result in greater interference when these conditions were met. When the conditions were not met, similarity would result in positive transfer. The tasks where Oller's conditions apply would normally be rigidly defined, with no tolerance of deviation from the straight and narrow path.
2. Almost 30 years ago Levelt made a highly relevant comparison of second language acquisition with other skills, emphasising that the starting proficiency for learning a related language is relatively high and that this initial advantage is maintained throughout learning:

    Interference is the negative side of an otherwise highly productive mechanism. The mechanism can be called 'transfer of training', and allows the organism to use automated patterns of activity in new tasks where conditions of performance and circumstances may be widely different: proficiency on the scooter may transfer to bicycle riding, skill in flute playing in learning to play the recorder, writing skill is easily transferred to blackboard writing though very different musculature is involved, etc. It is due to this productive mechanism that it is easier to learn a compatible language than a very unrelated language. From laboratory experiments it is clear that learning a new skill which is compatible with an existing skill is quicker than learning an incompatible skill. More exactly, the difference is not so much in the RATE of learning, but in the initial level of performance. The starting proficiency for a compatible activity is relatively high, and this initial advantage is maintained throughout learning. (Levelt, 1977: 61)

3. For a more detailed comparison between ball games and foreign language learning, see Ringbom (1987: 132). Johnson (1996) is an overview of the relationship between language learning/teaching and skills other than language. As he says (Johnson 1996: 177), the skills literature contains much interesting information that has not so far been considered in relation to language learning and teaching. See also Levelt (1975, 1977) and DeKeyser (2005).
4. The term monolingual should be used with care for Swedish-speaking Finns,

since even people who classify themselves as monolinguals have normally had several years of Finnish at school.

5. Although the immigrant setting is different from the foreign-language learning situation, it is worth noting that Mägiste (1984), who studied immigrants in Sweden, concluded that 'passive bilingualism' appears to facilitate learning a third language, whereas 'active bilingualism' might delay it.

Chapter 10
Development of Foreign Language Learning

In this chapter I will try to give an outline of how the development of foreign language learning could be described. My argumentation is based on three axioms:

(1) all learning of new knowledge and skills relates to previous knowledge and skills;
(2) item learning precedes system learning (see Cruttenden, 1981);
(3) comprehension precedes production.

None of these is very controversial in itself, though the distinction between items and systems is not familiar in SLA research.

These three axioms can be joined together in a more comprehensive approach to SLA in which the learner's development of the TL is not neglected. They can be combined by bringing in the concept of similarity (cross-linguistic as well as intralinguistic) as a guiding principle entering all three axioms.

If we disregard the preliminary stage of processing items for on-line comprehension, 'intake for communication' (see above, pp. 14ff.), which does not involve learning in the sense of a change in memory, we can distinguish four different types of learning: (1) item learning for comprehension, (2a) item learning for production, (2b) system learning for comprehension and (3) system learning for production. (See also Clark (1993: 245ff.) who distinguishes between C-representations (for comprehension) and P-representations (for production).) The reason for labelling the stages (2a) and (2b) rather than (2) and (3) is that these two normally develop in parallel, not successively.

Similarities can be perceived not only across related languages, but sometimes also across wholly unrelated languages. Occurrence of large numbers of high-frequency loanwords may facilitate vocabulary comprehension of English for speakers of very distant languages, such as Japanese (see above, p. 77). Swahili has taken over a substantial number of high-frequency loanwords from English, mainly key concepts in modern society (see Appendix 2).

Item Learning for Comprehension

Item learning for comprehension is the starting point, but how far can it take the learner? Cross-linguistic similarities are especially useful for learning to comprehend the new language: a fair receptive knowledge of a related TL can be attained quite quickly. If, on the other hand, there is a zero or near-zero similarity relation between the languages, the normal gap between receptive and productive vocabulary will be reduced, in that the acquisition of receptive competence takes a long time. The existence or absence of cross-linguistic similarities explains the difference in task magnitude between learning a related language and learning an unrelated one. Ultimately this difference goes back to the perception of how much and in what ways cross-linguistic similarities can be used for learning to comprehend words and underlying structures in the TL. Learners who can make use of positive transfer to facilitate learning to understand words in a new language can free many cognitive resources for other aspects of receptive learning (see also Odlin, 2003: 441).

Item Learning for Production

Item learning for production and system learning for comprehension follow the initial stage of item learning for comprehension. Usually there is a parallel development of these two, even though learners may primarily focus on either of them, depending on the aims, the learning situation, individual learner characteristics and so forth. In production of lexis, formal similarity between words may help in locating the intended L2-word. But errors are more likely to occur in production than in comprehension, partly because of the absence of a context ruling out wrong interpretations based on formal similarities. As has been said before, the learner attempting to produce L2, especially a distant L2, merely assumes cross-linguistic similarities, he does not perceive them. To convert receptive knowledge into productive knowledge requires a lot of time and practice, and this development is still not very well understood. The same is true of the relation between declarative knowledge and procedural knowledge.[1]

System Learning for Comprehension

System learning for comprehension means that oversimplified one-to-one relations are gradually modified. The learner learns, for example, that one L2-word can have several different meanings, that the past tense of verbs can be expressed by different morphemes and, in general, that pragmatic aspects of the target language are also relevant for learning. (For the pragmatic development in a second language, see Kasper and Rose, 2002.) There is also a development from partial towards precise understanding, and the learner expands the lexical network by learning more about the different sense relations a word has to other words (cf. Henriksen & Haastrup, 1998; Henriksen, 1999). Gradually an improved understanding develops of how different L2-units correspond to L1-units and/or how they relate to the underlying concepts. Cross-linguistic relations are not as easy to establish as in item learning, since the functional and semantic systems in two languages are reasonably congruent only in very closely related languages. In system learning, the cross-linguistic similarities are functional or semantic, while formal similarity plays a subordinate role, if any.

System Learning for Production

The final learning stage is system learning for production, and brings up the question of what kind of grammar the learner starts out from. It is neither the L1-grammar, nor the L2-grammar, but a very simple, minimally complex grammar that is gradually developed in the direction of the TL grammar (see Corder, 1983). Learners frequently produce utterances that are related neither to their L1-grammar nor to the TL grammar, and they also assume non-existent cross-linguistic similarities to their L1, which result in transfer-based errors even from a totally unrelated L1. (This has been discussed in the section on Grammar in Chapter 8.) George's (1972) concept of redundancy is helpful, as it is related to the learner's natural tendency to conserve effort (see Vildomec, 1963: 173). The role of redundancy is different in comprehension compared with production. The message of FL texts can be at least approximately comprehended even if some endings or function words are left unanalysed or unnoticed. For production, however, accuracy is required. If small words or endings are subconsciously regarded as 'less salient' and omitted, the result is errors that lead to reduced understanding or at least irritation in the listener. The learner has to realise this and make appropriate use of the many different linguistic means for expressing similar meanings; the learner also has to become aware that the same linguistic form can have several different functions or meanings. This applies to both grammar and vocabulary. In system learning for production, learners gradually learn to make use of their expanding lexical network. Known words are used in new senses, collocational restrictions are considered and links to other words are established. As learning progresses towards advanced proficiency, cross-linguistic similarity loses importance at the same time as intra-lingual similarity becomes more important.

The distinction made between learning for comprehension and learning for production does not mean that the processes of comprehension and production do not interact. Production normally presupposes at least some receptive knowledge. It is true that a learner may produce, for instance, a compound noun s/he afterwards says s/he has never met before (Faerch & Kasper, 1987). But the elements of the compound will have to be included in the learner's prior knowledge.

Near-native Proficiency

Only a small minority of learners achieve near-native proficiency, and when they do, they are in many respects similar to native speakers. When learners approach or reach this stage, the importance of cross-linguistic similarities recedes into the background. Even learners at a near-native stage make errors in foreign languages, and they particularly make use of words and constructions that cannot be categorically labelled as errors, but lie somewhere in the grey zone of acceptability. They are not really 'wrong', but they do not quite reflect how competent native speakers would best choose to express the message. 'Advanced learners' lexical problems are not due to a lack of vocabulary but rather to the inappropriate use of the words they know' (Meunier, 1998: 32).

The ICLE corpus (the International Corpus of Learner English) provides a great deal of valuable material written by university students of English (see, for example, Granger, 1998). Many, though clearly not all, of the essays produced by these writers approach near-nativeness. They include some words and constructions that can be clearly labelled as errors but, at least in some countries, this is not very frequent. Of the actual errors occurring in the corpora of Northern Europe, only a small minority can be referred back to L1-influence. Writers approaching near-nativeness do not generally reveal their L1 by using transfer-based words or constructions. They have reached a level of proficiency where the linguistic background of the writer, the role of transfer, has been pushed into the background, but where the linguistic resources of the TL are not used as fully or as adequately as by native writers. Word frequency studies reveal that even learners at a very advanced stage stick to Hasselgren's 'teddy bear principle': they tend to overuse words and phrases of a general nature and underuse the more specific, restricted phrasing favoured by native speakers (Lesniewska, 2006: 65; Ringbom, 1998). Non-nativeness in near-native writers will be most obvious when writers have to venture outside their own spheres of interest, and it tends to be revealed rather by lack of precision of phrasing and imperfect idiomaticity (see, for example, Bahns & Eldaw, 1993; Cobb,

2003; Ringbom, 1993: 295 ff, 1998). The use of collocations, in particular, is not always native-like, and tends to lag behind the learners' general knowledge of vocabulary (Bahns & Eldaw, 1993: 101). The non-native cultural and educational background of advanced L2-writers may also be seen in analyses of the argumentative structure of texts. Studies referring to Finnish writers of argumentative or academic English include Connor (1987, 1996); Crismore *et al.* (1993); Mauranen (1993) (see also Ingberg, 1987; Isaksson-Wikberg, 1999). Idioms are an area where there is a marked contrast between an advanced learner's uncertainty and the confident intuition and experience of the native speaker (Cornell, 1999; Mäntylä, 2004).

If learners at near-native level write about topics they know well, their non-native elements may be kept to a minimum. In fact, native speakers often find it hard to distinguish native from near-native texts (Ringbom, 1993, Waller, 1993). In speaking, disguising non-native features is more difficult. A slightly foreign intonation normally reveals to a perceptive listener the non-nativeness of even an advanced learner, and yet more important clues as to non-nativeness are provided by gaps in a foreign language learner's pragmatic knowledge. In the end it may even be an advantage for the truly proficient foreign language learner to retain at least a slight foreign accent. If a learner is too native-like in his production, inevitable pragmatic errors involve a risk that he will be regarded as a stupid native rather than as an intelligent foreigner. Alan Davies (1994: 148) makes the same point: 'It is possible to perform too well in a foreign language ... A foreign accent may be a good badge to display – "don't expect me to share all your cultural assumptions!"' This of course does not mean that teaching should not *aim* at truly native-like proficiency.

Notes

1. Some researchers, above all Krashen, have maintained that declarative (analytical) knowledge is of little or no use to the L2 learner. This may be true for some learners in some learning situations, but it is clearly dangerous to generalize on this.

Chapter 11
Consequences for Teaching

The EuroCom Project

The Scandinavian situation, where the languages are mutually comprehensible, eliminates (or at least reduces the need for) teaching, since the
speaker of one Scandinavian language can make good use of its obvious
cross-linguistic similarities to the neighbouring languages. How to identify
not-so-obvious cross-linguistic similarities and describe them in a way that
is fruitful to learners is a challenge that has recently been taken up by the
EuroCom project. The main aim of the project is to produce textbooks and
other material that makes use of the facilitative potential for reading
comprehension inherent in speakers of languages that are related, but are
not so close as to be mutually comprehensible. For inter-European communication, EuroCom proposes not a lingua franca, but, along the lines
suggested by Umberto Eco among many others, the development of a
partial linguistic competence in as many languages as possible. EuroCom
convincingly argues the advantages of making use of cross-linguistic similarities. The main focus so far has been on achieving reading knowledge in
the Romance languages, and the initiative has come from speakers of
German.[1] A number of EuroCom publications, with a practical didactic
aim, have appeared recently. McCann, *et al.* (2003) is a modified translation
of Klein and Stegmann (2000) catering for English speakers, and among
other publications may be mentioned Meissner and Reinfried (1998) and
Reinfried (1999). In these books, similarities and affinities are used to
facilitate above all reading comprehension across Romance languages.
What EuroCom also needs is a thorough theoretically-grounded discussion of the ways in which cross-linguistic similarities work across related
languages. Some theoretical aspects of European inter-comprehension are
set out in Stoye (2000); see also Klein (2002).

The basic idea of EuroCom is simple. If you know one Romance
language you already have a lot of relevant knowledge that can be used for
understanding the others. The learner is helped on the way by descriptions
of what are called 'The Seven Sieves', where systematic correspondences
between all Romance languages are set out. The seven sieves are (1) international vocabulary; (2) pan-Romance vocabulary; (3) sound correspondences;

(4) spelling and pronunciation; (5) syntactic structures; (6) morphosyntax; and (7) affixes.

Though there are speakers of Romance languages who have learned to read another Romance language without external guidance, the number can surely be dramatically increased with the proper guidance of EuroCom textbooks. For listening, the task will be much more demanding, but not impossible (see Meissner & Burk, 2001). At any rate, it is encouraging to find that serious efforts are now at last being made to make practical use of the facilitative learning potential that exists between speakers of related languages. Work has recently begun on applying the same principles to Germanic languages. The project is led by Britta Hufeisen (see Duke *et al.*, 2004; Hufeisen, 2005) and will use EuroCom ideas and principles to facilitate intercomprehension of not only the most commonly spoken Germanic languages, but also the two official Norwegian languages, Bokmål and Nynorsk, as well as Icelandic, Frisian and Faeroese. Some of these may exhibit differences more concrete than those across the Romance languages, and might therefore pose problems, but EuroComGerm is a commendable enterprise deserving all the support it can get. German is the central language for all EuroCom publications, and native or near-native knowledge of German is, if not necessary, at least highly desirable, for efficient use of the material. As the work on EuroComGerm has only recently begun, it is at this stage focusing on German as both bridge language and language of communication. This clearly restricts the number of potential users of EuroComGerm material. Future works having English as the main bridge language and language of communication will no doubt lead to the wide recognition the project deserves, since English has the unchallenged position as the non-native language best known in the world.

Teaching the Use of Learning Strategies

Cross-linguistic similarity is an important variable in the use of learning strategies: how the learner tries to enhance the effectiveness of learning. Whether foreign language instruction should actively encourage and teach about beneficial learning strategies is a matter frequently debated in recent years. How effective learning strategies are depends on a large number of variables, such as 'proficiency level, task, text, language modality, background knowledge, context of learning, target language and learner characteristics' (Chamot & Rubin, 1994: 772). A lot of research is therefore needed to find out about the interplay of these variables, and the question is further complicated by uncertainty about how a learning strategy should be defined (cf. Dörnyei & Skehan, 2004: 607ff.).

Though detailed studies are needed, there seems to be fairly general agreement among researchers regarding the general usefulness of instruction in learning strategies. Attention to cross-linguistic similarities provides the basis for the use of many cognitive and metacognitive strategies, as the following quotations indicate:

- 'Systematically pointing out the most frequent "sound correspondences" ... between (in this case) English and Dutch proved to be very effective' (Schouten-van Parreren, 1989: 81).
- 'Various ways of encouraging increased strategic processing through instruction can be beneficial' (Harley, 1995: 19).
- 'Teachers can reduce the learning burden of grammatical patterns by showing learners where English usage parallels mother-tongue usage, by avoiding vocabulary items which take unpredictable patterns, and by showing learners useful parallel patterns in English' (Nation, 1990: 37).

Learning strategies for comprehension are not the same as learning strategies for production. And learning strategies at the early stages of learning differ from those at later stages: learners gradually develop different strategies. As Meara (1988: 13) has indicated the vocabulary acquisition processes of reasonably proficient learners are not very different from those of adolescent native speakers. Longitudinal studies are needed for a better understanding of the underlying processes. If instruction is given, it should be adjusted to the different stages of learning. Initially, the strategies taught might primarily aim at simplifying the learning task but, when learning progresses, the strategies might be better aimed at expanding and deepening already acquired knowledge. The movement from item learning to system learning has parallels in the learning strategies used. Swan makes a relevant point:

The more aware learners are of the similarities and differences between their mother tongue and the target language, the easier they will find it to adopt effective learning and production strategies. Informed teaching can help students to formulate realistic hypotheses about the nature and limits of cross-linguistic correspondences and to become more attentive to important categories in the second language which have no mother-tongue counterpart. (Swan 1997: 179)

Lexical cross-linguistic similarities provide the most concrete material on which learners can employ effective learning strategies. An extensive taxonomy of vocabulary learning strategies is given by Schmitt (1997), and it is easy to see that the variables relevant to effective strategies vary considerably from one learning situation to another. Schmitt's taxonomy is based on a study of Japanese learners and in many of his strategies cross-linguistic aspects do not enter the picture. Where the perceived distance between the L1 and the TL is closer than between Japanese and English, cross-linguistic similarities will increase in importance. But even for Japanese learners of English, where a major problem for the teacher is how to make the learners overcome the phonological differences between *gairaigo* and English (see above, p. 77), reliance on cross-linguistic similarities must be regarded as an aid, not an obstacle.

One reason for this comes from what is known from cognitive psychology: that deeper involvement in manipulation of information leads to more effective learning (Schmitt, 1997: 201; see also Marton, 1977: 48). Paying attention to both meaning and the formal properties of the TL has also been found to be one characteristic of good language learners (see further the survey of the good language learner studies in R. Ellis, 1995: 546). Haastrup's points about lexical inferencing are also relevant here:

(1) If words are acquired through inferencing + feedback, they are better retained than words acquired through presentation + formal practice.
(2) If a word is acquired in a low-predictable context, i.e. inferencing procedures have involved the use of linguistic cues, it is better retained than items the meaning of which is inferred on the basis of contextual cues. (Haastrup, 1991: 320)

In some circumstances, TL similarities to languages other than L1 should also be taken into account and put to good use.

Metalinguistic awareness can be increased through teaching similarities between languages. Multilingual education should therefore concentrate on increasing metalinguistic awareness in language students by teaching commonalities among languages they already know. An increased focus on similarities could offer positive effects for multilingual education. This perspective would also imply the reactivation of the knowledge of other languages in the learner and thus prior knowledge could guide learners in the development of a further language system. (Jessner, 1999: 207)

Jessner's point about the usefulness of languages other than the L1 is clearly relevant for comprehension. As for production, there will probably be real advantages only, or primarily, for those L3-learners who have acquired a reasonable proficiency in L2.

Haastrup's point about the teacher's role is well taken:

What we can do is to increase learners' awareness of available knowledge sources, sensitise them to the concept of linguistic similarity, encourage them always to check their hypotheses at top level and remember that all languages have polysemes. The teacher's most difficult task is to strike a balance between encouraging transfer and instilling transfer-anxiety in her students. (Haastrup, 1991: 341)

One major obstacle to overcome in successful research on the relevance of instruction to the improvement of learning strategies is 'to discover how second language teachers can be trained to provide learning strategy instruction to their students' (O'Malley & Chamot, 1990: 186).

More generally, the situation in research on the relevance of instruction to developing efficient learning strategies brings to mind the simple axiom that we need to know enough about learning before we start making assumptions on the efficiency of teaching. The literature on language teaching methodology is full of examples of how the supposed excellence of a certain method or approach is actually based on unfounded assumptions of how learning comes about.

The Relevance of Cross-linguistic Similarities for Teaching English to Finnish and Finland-Swedish Learners

In learning English, Swedish speakers are not faced with such big problems as Finnish speakers. The two language groups employ different learning strategies that depend on the differences in their prior linguistic knowledge. At early stages of learning, teachers at Finland-Swedish schools might succeed in making full use of the cross-linguistic similarities between English and Swedish. Even though the regular one-to-one correspondences that can be established in item learning are often oversimplified, they provide a useful and concrete start for the learner, and the oversimplification will gradually wear off as learning progresses. After a very elementary knowledge of English grammar has been achieved, mere examples, not grammar rules in themselves, may often be sufficient for developing a basic linguistic accuracy in Swedes. It seems that Swedes can make effective use of implicit learning, which 'is at its best when only concrete and contiguous elements are involved' (DeKeyser, 2003: 319).

Perhaps the main problem for teachers of English in Swedish schools is the complacency of students. The relative ease with which a receptive knowledge and an elementary communicative competence of English, with its simple morphology, can be achieved very easily leads to the attitude 'I can't be bothered to work on English, I'll manage anyway.' There are many opportunities for learning English outside the classroom, but the type of language learnt through extra-curricular activities (especially from TV programmes, music and computers), differs from what is taught in class, and teachers need to be fully aware of these differences. Forsman (2004) is a study of the knowledge and attitudes of Finland-Swedish teenagers which pays particular attention to the type of English learnt outside class. Mainly, it is the receptive skills that are learnt through outside activities. As far as production goes, many Finland-Swedish students simply are not prepared to expend energy on expanding their active vocabulary and acquiring a more-than-basic writing ability. Cross-linguistic similarities facilitate learning, especially learning for comprehension, but they may also lull learners into thinking that learning is easy and that they already know as much as they need of the TL. This means that less effort will go into learning. To merely pass the Matriculation Examination in English does not require much effort from an average student with Swedish as L1, but the goal of teaching should not be set too low for Swedish schools. Learning to speak and write any new language really well requires hard work, and teachers need to fight the complacency they often encounter in the classroom. Similar student attitudes will no doubt also be found in the neighbouring Scandinavian countries, and if Swedish-speaking Finns at the upper secondary level have been found to do slightly better than their Scandinavian peers this could be put down to their bilingual background. By any international standards, Swedish-speaking Finns in Finland start out from a very favourable position for learning English. They can perceive many concrete cross-linguistic similarities, and most of them have a strong metalinguistic awareness since they already know a language other than their L1 when they begin to learn English in the classroom. Further, coming from a small country where English has a high status, they generally have a strong motivation for learning it. But affirmation of a higher standard than that in the neighbouring Scandinavian countries would require a thorough investigation of the complex variables relevant for comparative investigations. Information would be needed, not only on the number of classroom hours, but also on how much time learners spend on English outside the classroom. And the very best Finland-Swedish students (those who go on to study English as a university subject) have been found to be at a lower, rather than at a higher, level than their peers at Scandinavian universities as far as vocabulary knowledge is concerned (Engberg, 1993; Zettersten, 1979).

As for Finnish learners, it should be noted that the standard of English proficiency as reflected in the Matriculation Examination clearly seems to have improved during the last two decades. Partly this is a subjective impression formed during almost 30 years as an examiner, but the good results achieved in recent international evaluations speak for themselves.[2] Thirty years ago Finnish teenagers would hardly have produced better results in an English comprehension test than Danes (see above, pp. 49ff.). The teaching of English in Finland at that time was firmly based on the grammar–translation method. Also, Finnish society was much more isolated than its Scandinavian counterparts, with relatively few influences from abroad. Nowadays at least the bigger cities probably vary little from Scandinavian communities of the same size. A few caveats are needed, however. Rural schools were not tested in the Scandinavian INS project, only schools in Helsinki and Vaasa, and on the whole Finnish schools in the countryside and small towns do not do at all as well in the Matriculation Examination in English as schools in the bigger cities. Also, it must be remembered that the INS (*internordisk språkförståelse*, the inter-Nordic language comprehension) project tested only comprehension, not production.

Compared with Swedes, however, Finns are at a disadvantage in comprehension, since there are, as it were, very few 'magnets' – items formally similar to English that attract new items contributing to the building of an extensive associative L2 network for receptive competence. In foreign language learners, this network is very largely based on formal similarities. Finns have to devote considerable effort both to create such a network and to learn to understand elements of English linguistic structure that are unfamiliar to them. They realise that a lot of work is required from a learner: they learn discipline from the very start of their studies. This is in fact perfectly in line with what the classics Sweet (1899/1964: 54f.) and Palmer (1917/1968: 33f.) had already said (see also Ringbom, 1987: 44ff.).

James also has a relevant comment here:

> What is important (in the difference between learning related and unrelated languages) is not so much the facilitation that comes from early comprehension, as the learners' encounter with problematicity in the early stages of learning a distant language. This forces them to attend to the minutiae of form in order to understand. This in turn necessitates that they learn the L2 grammar and rely less on guessing (or 'top-down processing') and it instils in learners an accuracy-consciousness that will stay with them and will curb their excessive 'linguistic adventurism'. (James, 1993: 15)

Finns simply have to devote more time to understanding the structure of English, i.e. they need to find out about the grammatical structure of the language; in practice, this often means having to learn explicitly formulated rules. This provides an important reason why accuracy rather than fluency has traditionally been emphasised in Finnish schools. Earlier overemphasis on accuracy has, it seems, now been superseded by a generally reasonable balance between accuracy, i.e. mainly knowledge of grammar, and fluency, the ability to cope in comprehension and (written) production. A swing of the pendulum can be observed: today it seems that focusing on grammatical form is no longer regarded as an unnecessary burden in foreign language teaching, as was often thought in some quarters 20-30 years ago. Learners, of course, are different: while some do not want to hear anything about grammar rules, others, especially adult learners, definitely want to pay attention to grammatical form and develop their understanding of how the TL works. What has not often been said in so many words is that psychotypology is relevant to what proportion of time teaching should devote to grammar. The more distant the TL is to the L1, the more necessary it is to pay attention to grammatical structures, especially when written production is emphasised. Finding the right balance between the ideals of fluency and accuracy is something language teachers always have to bear in mind. But, as Meara has said, a grammar-based approach to the syllabus where learners acquire only a limited vocabulary allows students to operate 'reasonably well within a classroom context, where the lexical environment is very limited and very predictable. Outside this protected environment, however, they are often unable to cope' (Meara, 1995: 8). The good results of Finnish learners of English in an international perspective have not involved tests of oral production, and it has so far not been possible to include oral production as a compulsory part of the Matriculation Examination, although an optional test has been operating in recent years.

In Finland, oral production is clearly the weakest area in English proficiency. While the results of international evaluations of comprehension present a flattering picture of Finns' knowledge of English, the European Commission's survey into what percentage of the populations can participate in an English conversation reveals something quite different. Only 50% of Finns can do that, while the percentage for Denmark, Sweden and Holland is about 75 (Hufeisen, 2005). Other figures present the same picture. According to Pietiläinen (2005), who relies on figures from Eurobarometer 54 Special from 2001, 31% of the Finnish population speak no language other than their L1. The equivalent figures for Sweden, Denmark and Holland are under 15%. A somewhat rosier picture is given by Takala (2002), who quotes the figures given by the Finnish Central Board of Statistics. In the year 2000, the figure for the purely monolingual Finns was estimated to be 22%. Takala (2000: 275) also mentions that Finns tend to evaluate their own foreign language proficiency more critically than many other countries do.

One specific criticism of 'Finglish' has focused on the staccato speech and the tendency of transferring 'the habit of pronouncing all of the sylla-bles of each word unreduced and manifesting word boundaries with phonetical juncture segments (instead of linking)' (Lehtonen, 1979: 45). Insufficient automatisation of speech procedures is no doubt more common in speaking languages unrelated to the L1. It is also tempting to link this to the stereotype of the taciturn Finn. Finnish people are generally considered shy and reticent by people from Central European, Mediterra-nean and Anglo-American cultures. A popular postcard provided carica-tures of characteristic stereotypes of each EU member nation (German humour, British cooking and the sober Irishman). The perfect European was described as being as 'talkative as a Finn' and the accompanying illus-tration showed a couple of people with their mouths closed with adhesive tape. The self-image of the Finns is largely similar: that of a taciturn, stub-born people with low social competence. Studies by Lehtonen and Sajavaara (most recently Sajavaara & Lehtonen, 1997) and Lehtonen (2002) provide illuminating discussions of 'the silent Finn', placing the character-istics in a wider cultural context.

It is clear that Finnish attitudes and Finnish behaviour have changed recently and are all the time opening up. The pace of change is, however, slow. Frequent negative experiences of foreigners living or staying in Finland still focus on their problems of communication, usually in English, with Finns. But these problems are clearly not primarily problems of language proficiency, since many of these foreign guests speak worse English than their Finnish hosts do. They are problems of general, cultur-ally-bound social and communicational skills. Even in advanced learners generally, socio-pragmatic competence lags behind linguistic competence, and this seems to hold true especially in Finland. For many Finns socio-pragmatic competence is often relatively undeveloped and their shortcom-ings are heightened in cross-cultural communication. Teaching these aspects with special emphasis on cross-cultural communication would be important, not only for schools, but for any work place where people from other cultures are found.

At least in the older generation, apprehensive attitudes to speaking foreign languages are in part a result of the earlier situation in Finnish schools, where authoritarian attitudes prevailed for a long time. The monopoly status of translation in the Matriculation Examination produced an exaggerated emphasis on accuracy and a corresponding neglect of fluency. The translations were marked according to an intricate system of weighed minus points for each error (see Enkvist, 1973). There can be no doubt that this often led to a general uneasy fear of making errors, and a dominant attitude, particularly among people who today have reached at least middle age, was that one should not try to speak another language if one could not do it really well.[3] To what extent apprehensiveness in speaking foreign languages still remains should be investigated further, but certainly young people in the larger cities today do not shy away from speaking English in the way that their parents' generation did.

Finns can perceive relatively few concrete similarities between English and Finnish, but if strategies to make use of those similarities that do exist were taught, learning might well be facilitated at least to some extent (for structural similarities, see Seppänen (1998) and above, p. 12). If cross-linguistic similarities are exaggerated at the earliest stages of learning, this will make for facilitation of learning, even if it also results in some inaccuracies, which will normally be adjusted as learning progresses.

The picture that consistently emerges from a large number of studies shows the expected clear differences within Finland between Swedish and Finnish learners in favour of the Swedes. A natural question following from the general advantages of Swedish learners of English is whether a non-native knowledge of a related language also helps and whether teaching should encourage parallels to be drawn between non-native languages. It is, however, doubtful whether similarities between English and non-native Swedish should be stressed in English teaching in Finnish-language schools. Making use of their knowledge of a related non-native language would almost certainly be helpful for those L3 learners who are bilingual or have already reached good fluency in their L2, but such learners are in a clear minority in Finnish classrooms. Nowadays, they are somewhat more likely to be found in Swedish lessons, where there are often at least a few students who have reached a good standard of proficiency in English at an early stage. The students in English lessons, on the other hand, generally have a poor or non-existent knowledge of Swedish. Exceptions may be provided by a few classrooms in bilingual areas along the coast, and probably some or most of the 4% of Finnish learners who have opted for starting Swedish, rather than English, at the age of 9. Without good L2 proficiency and/or well-developed linguistic thinking, English and Swedish can be difficult to keep apart for an ordinary teenage learner. But if a teacher can provide selected cognitive-based training in L2–L3 similarities, it will probably aid learners in their comprehension of L3 (Marx, 2005).

The more similar to the L1 that a target language is perceived to be, the more teaching can concentrate on the differences there are. Listening comprehension and vocabulary differences will be in the foreground if the languages are so close (including structurally) that written texts are almost or on the whole mutually comprehensible. Learners can then fairly soon go on to increase their vocabulary through extensive reading where they can infer the approximate meaning of unknown words. It is by such incidental acquisition that vocabulary learning generally occurs after the first few thousand most common words (Huckin & Coady, 1999: 182). Learning for comprehension of a language perceived to be similar requires little effort, and if you already have a receptive knowledge it must be much easier to convert it into productive knowledge than trying to acquire productive knowledge, as it were, from scratch. If, on the other hand, the TL has few borrowings from or cognates with the L1 or some other language the learner knows, the learner first needs to devote a lot of effort in acquiring a sufficiently large basic receptive vocabulary. Only then will s/he be able to make effective use of the reading strategies learners apply in incidental vocabulary acquisition through reading. In classrooms, the teacher's guiding role is important. 'Appropriate teaching can help learners to develop realistic equivalence hypotheses, appropriate compensatory strategies and an understanding of the nature of error' (Swan, 1997: 180).

The consequence of the emphasis on learning for comprehension in this book might seem to favour an approach to language teaching where the students are not asked to produce anything in the foreign language until they have acquired a fairly extensive receptive knowledge. According to this approach, learners can benefit from greater receptive exposure to the target language. An early concentration on developing receptive skills, leading to a solid receptive knowledge, is an excellent basis for the development of productive skills. Early emphasis on L2 vocabulary, as proposed by Meara (1995), fits in well with this approach. The transfer effects from reception to production can hardly be contested, even if the details of how this comes about are still unclear. Delayed Oral Production was an approach advocated especially in the 1970s and it produced promising results in some situations (see, for example, Asher, 1977; N.F. Davies, 1978; Nord, 1976; Postovsky, 1974). When you learn a typologically distant language, comprehension develops slowly, and in Finnish schools it might be a promising idea to combat that by focusing on comprehension at the early stages of learning. Practising language teachers in Finland have, however, not really warmed to this idea, if they are at all familiar with it, and a great deal of work would certainly be involved for the teachers in developing the required extensive batteries of comprehension tests. We probably have to wait until some enthusiastic teachers or teacher trainers want to start experimenting with this method, but reform initiatives originating from the classroom floor are not particularly common in Finland. For experiments with new methods and approaches to be successful, they generally have to originate with people who are themselves actively engaged in language teaching.

Notes

1. That the main impetus as well as the main activity of a project focusing on Romance languages should be located in Germany brings to mind the point made about the relevance of a thorough L2 knowledge of Finnish for learning Swahili (p. 79 and Appendix 2). The German interest in learning several Romance languages might be another indication that learners of an additional language after L2 may profit more from an extensive declarative L2 knowledge of a language perceived to be similar to the target language than if the knowledge derives from the learner's intuitive mastery of L1. This would obviously be a matter for EuroCom to look into.

2. Schools in Finland also do well in subjects other than English. Recent international comparisons in reading and mathematics (the PISA study, investigating 200,000 15-year-olds in more than 40 countries) have shown that Finnish schools are at the top of the list in these topics – in spite of Finnish teenagers being found to have a much more negative attitude to school than their peers in Scandinavian countries. Many reasons have been given for this success; see, for example, Linnakylä & Välijärvi (2003). The Finnish nation was built up with the aid of education from the start, school and education are generally highly valued by parents, the culture is relatively homogeneous with relatively few immigrants, the quality of teacher education is good, and the teaching profession is probably valued more highly than in most Western countries. Schools also pay special attention to weak pupils, and the level of achievement in different schools varies very little. What may seem paradoxical is that these same Finnish 15-year-olds have a much more negative attitude to school than their peers in Scandinavia, though this might be due to a slightly more authoritarian system in Finland than in the neighbouring countries, which in its turn might possibly increase rather than decrease efficiency of learning. What may or may not be relevant here is also the result of recent investigations of mental health in the Nordic countries. Teenagers in Finland are apparently more depressed than their peers in Sweden and Norway.

3. Translation in itself cannot be regarded as a bad type of language test, if it is combined with other types. Rather it was the monopoly of translation in the Matriculation Examination that essentially produced attitudes promoting speech anxiety in foreign language learners. Lindros (1987) describes the situation in the early 1980s, comparing Finnish and Finland Swedish university students. Making use of a questionnaire, he found that there was relatively little apprehension in, and hardly any differences between, students of English at Jyväskylä University (Finnish-speaking students) and at Åbo Akademi University (Swedish-speaking students). There was much more apprehension in students of political science, and the Jyväskylä students were also more apprehensive in their use of English than Åbo Akademi students were. The least apprehension (even lower than in the students of English) was found in the small group of Finnish-speaking political science students studying at Åbo Akademi. They were a highly select group who had already shown absence of language apprehension by opting to study at a university in a language other than their L1.

Chapter 12
Further Research Needed

Development from Receptive to Productive Competence

What happens when a receptive competence becomes activated for production is a topic which is not well understood? In 1979, Levenston was already criticising the oversimplified binary distinction between active/ productive and passive/receptive knowledge of vocabulary. Melka and Meara both provide some useful insights in Schmitt and McCarthy (1997). In Meara's words:

> The crucial distinction between active and passive vocabulary might simply be that active vocabulary items are connected to their parent lexicons by more than one type of connection. Clearly, if this idea is correct, then the encounter situation that allows the first connection *from* L (= lexicon) *to* W (= word) to be established will have the effect of turning W from a passive/receptive item to an active/productive one. (Meara, 1997: 119)

Having reached a basic receptive competence, what the learner especially needs in order to be successful at producing the language fluently is a strong drive to communicate and interact, leading to a lot of practice in using the language. But the details of this development are not clear:

> It is still very unresolved in vocabulary research how we are to define the difference between receptive and productive competence of a specific lexical item (a) as a difference between input/output modules and specifications (Nick Ellis, 1994); (b) as a difference between the type and extent of automaticity which has been developed; or (c) as a difference in the type i.e. the quality of meaning representation a lexical item has in our mental lexicon. (Henriksen & Haastrup, 1998: 68)

The development of grammatical competence from receptive to productive has received even less attention than lexical aspects, since SLA research on grammar has tended to deal with productive, but not with receptive competence.

Cross-linguistic vs. Intralinguistic Similarities

Cross-linguistic and intralinguistic similarities may, at least in theory, be easy to distinguish for the analyst, but the distinction need not be salient for learners. In fact, learners may well look for formal item similarity wherever they see a chance of finding it, regardless of whether the TL form relates to L1 or to another form in the TL. The same psychological process, searching for similarities, especially formal similarities, is involved in both. The distinctions that *are* important are those between comprehension and production, and between formal and functional/semantic similarity. When learners, especially in the early stages, are trying to establish one-to-one cross-linguistic equivalences, they are primarily concerned with perceiving formal similarities between items. Functional similarities to L1 are what the learner expects, and when his expectations are not met, as will occur in the learning of languages perceived to be distant, delays in learning are inevitable.

James (1998: 184ff.) lists the causes of errors due to the target language (intralinguistic errors) and distinguishes between learning-strategy based errors and communication-strategy based errors. He emphasises the problems of error diagnosis but concludes that there is no easy alternative to tackling it head-on (James, 1998: 203).

Longitudinal Studies

Psychologists make much use of longitudinal studies in L1 acquisition, but in transfer-related research on SLA it is not very common to follow one or two learners for any length of time. However, the work by Hammarberg and Williams (1993), Williams and Hammarberg (1998) and Hammarberg (2001) provides an interesting exception in its description of the gradual switch from L2 transfer to L1 transfer in one L3 learner. Still, more investigations are clearly needed.

Chapter 13

Conclusion

Previous studies have already shown without doubt that Swedish speakers have a great advantage, compared with Finnish speakers, in learning English. Essentially, the difference is not a difference in speed of learning, but a difference in starting levels. Even before learning starts, Swedes have a great deal of relevant knowledge of English. In their initial encounter with the language, their L1-based expectations of what the TL is like turn out to be largely justified.

This work has provided details of how and where the differences between the two language groups are manifested and has tried to show the reasons for these differences. The discussion may be clarified by considering important distinctions related to the learning process: the three different types of cross-linguistic similarity relations – similarity, contrast and zero. The different consequences of these relations in respect to item learning and system learning, comprehension and production have been discussed, and a distinction between perceived and assumed similarities has been proposed.

Cross-linguistic similarity is obviously not the only factor influencing SLA, but it is an extremely important one that has hitherto not been accorded the attention it deserves in research. Good language learners especially make efficient use of whatever cross-linguistic similarities they perceive.

In learning for comprehension, cross-linguistic item similarities to L1 can normally be perceived, unless the languages are very distant from each other. Although some similarities may turn out to be merely apparent, or at any rate oversimplified, such perceived item similarities are overwhelmingly facilitative and give rise to positive transfer. The more correspondences to L1 that can be made, the more facilitation of learning there is. Similarities across low-frequency items, usually manifested as loanwords, are of less use than similarities across high-frequency items. If item similarities cannot be perceived, the learner has to be content with merely assuming similarities. More often than not, these assumed similarities lead the learner astray, causing errors especially in production.

In contrast to item similarities, which may be either perceived or assumed, system similarities are merely assumed, at least in the early stages of learning. The degree of congruence between the systems, i.e. whether and to what extent L1 procedures also work for L2, determines how much facilitation there will be in learning for comprehension. Closely-related languages have very similar, though not identical systems and are largely based on the same organisational principles. When you learn to comprehend a language related to your L1, the assumption that the procedures work more or less in the same way as in L1 is generally justified. Across totally unrelated languages, on the other hand, there is little or no facilitation: few L2 items have similar equivalents in the L1, and L1 procedures for L2 comprehension work only to a limited extent or not at all.

In learning for production, both item and system similarities are merely assumed, but assumption can be, and often is, based on previous perception during learning for comprehension. It is not always easy to see the distinction between perception and assumption, since there is constant interaction between the two, but the situation is clearer across distant languages, when few or no similarities can be perceived, and the learner's application of transfer works on the basis of more or less unfounded assumptions. Assumption of system similarities gives rise to procedural transfer, and although there is positive procedural transfer, it is difficult for an observer to recognise, and the procedural transfer has therefore frequently been seen to have consistently negative effects.

The differences here outlined between learning related and unrelated languages apply mainly to the early stages of learning. As learning progresses, learners of both related and unrelated languages learn to apply strategies and processes that are more TL native-like, and the difference between the two types of learners gradually diminishes. The different magnitudes of the task of learning are obvious for comprehension, and it is hoped that the consequences of this difference will be more clearly understood also for production. Learning for comprehension is in important ways different from learning for production.

For a closely-related target language, cross-linguistic similarities can not only be assumed, they can be perceived at an early stage, thus facilitating comprehension and learning for comprehension. Potential knowledge across languages perceived to be similar is converted into real knowledge, and items can be learnt and retrieved for comprehension. Quick and effective item learning for comprehension, facilitated by cross-linguistic structural similarities, is above all what distinguishes the learning of a related target language from learning an unrelated language. If the organisational principles of L1 do not apply to the TL, comprehension and learning will be delayed. We should not talk about similarity vs. difference; for the learner it is a question of similarity vs. absence of similarity, which is not the same thing. From the very beginning of learning, the process of looking for similarities is in the learner's focus. To what degree the search is successful is fundamental for learners: establishing differences is something secondary.

Cross-linguistic similarity facilitates automatisation of procedures, and is therefore particularly useful for the oral skills of listening and speaking, where quick and efficient retrieval of relevant items is required.

Appendix 1

Deceptive English–Swedish Cognates

The following is a list of those English cognates that can be considered particularly dangerous for the Swedish-speaking learner, in that they tend to occur in similar contexts but have different meanings (Ringbom, 1995). A more complete list of deceptive cognates can be compiled from the three studies by Ekblom (1933), Ernolv (1958) and Hargevik and Stevens (1978).

English	Swedish		English	Swedish	
actual	*aktuell*	'topical'	overtake	*överta*	'take over'
blank	*blank*	'shiny'	phoney	*fånig*	'silly'
blithe	*blid*	'mild, gentle'	plump	*plump*	'vulgar'
companion	*kompanjon*	'partner'	sensible	*sensibel*	'sensitive'
consequent	*konsekvent*	'consistent'	sham	*skam*	'shame'
crafty	*kraftig*	'strong'	slump	*slump*	'chance'
eventually	*eventuellt*	'possibly'	spiritual	*spirituell*	'witty'
foul	*ful*	'ugly'	sticky	*stickig*	'prickly'
genial	*genial*	'ingenious'	thrifty	*driftig*	'energetic'
lusty	*lustig*	'funny'	warehouse	*varuhus*	'dept. store'
map	*mapp*	'folder'	wink	*vinka*	'beckon'
musty	*mustig*	'aromatic'	wrist	*vrist*	'ankle, instep'

Appendix 2

'If you know Finnish as L2, there will be no major problem learning Swahili.'

The above statement was uttered by Knut Pipping, a multilingual Swedish-speaking academic in Finland (1920–1998) in connection with his paper on Swahili presented at the Åbo Akademi Linguistics Society in the 1970s, immediately after his two-year stay as visiting Professor of Sociology in Tanzania. His language background was Swedish L1, Finnish L2 (near-native with a thorough theoretical school background), German, English and Dutch (fluent, possibly near-native).

Swahili, a Bantu language used as the medium of communication in large parts of East Africa, is spoken by nearly 70 million people. Though no genetic relationship exists between Finnish and Swahili, there are resemblances in their structure. Above all both are highly agglutinative languages, where numerous word affixes can be joined to the word stem. The words are long, and the word as linguistic unit takes on a different significance from what it has in the Germanic languages. There is considerable morphemic and morpho-phonemic variation in both languages and they are both also highly vowel-dominant. There are hardly any prepositions and only a few postpositions, and grammatical concord is essential. There is also a distinction between case endings of the object. By means of different affixes Swahili distinguishes whether the object indicates the whole or part of something, just as Finnish does.

Some random sentences in Swahili, Finnish and English (Table 9) illustrate the different numbers of words used.

As for vocabulary, many of the nouns basic to a modern society have been borrowed into Swahili from English, and thus even a relatively superficial knowledge of English will also aid an attentive learner with an open mind (*tikiti* – ticket, *gari* – car, *keki* – cake (Finnish *kakku*), *daktari* – doctor (Finnish *tohtori*), *baisikeli* – bicycle, *stempu* – stamp, *treni* – train, *hospitali* – hospital, *lori* – lorry, *shule* – school, *sukari* – sugar (Finnish *sokeri*). Another parallel between Finnish and Swahili is that some loanwords from English are introduced into both languages simply by adding an *i* (bus – Swahili *basi*, Finnish *bussi*; mile – Swahili *maili*, Finnish *maili*).

Table 9

Swahili	Finnish	English
Utasafisha meza?	*Puhdistatko pöydän?*	Will you clean the table?
Nilisahau kununua tikiti.	*Unohdin ostaa lipun.*	I forgot to buy the ticket.
Tusipopata gari hatusafiri.	*Jos emme saa autoa, emme matkusta.*	If we can't get a car, we shan't travel.
Tutaonana na mwalimu kesho.	*Tapaamme huomenna opettajan kanssa.*	We are going to meet with the teacher tomorrow.
Nilimwona mwalimu mjini.	*Näin opettajan kaupungilla.*	I saw the teacher in town.
Alimzuia mtoto astembee njiani.	*Hän esti lasta kävelemästä tiellä.*	He prevented the child from walking on the road.

Source: Hurskainen (2000)

Pipping's thorough declarative L2 knowledge of Finnish, not L1 knowledge, probably helped him more than L1 knowledge would. Native speakers, unless they have made a close study of their L1 or are unusually intelligent or creative, normally have great problems explaining to foreign learners *why* something has to be expressed in the way it is expressed. A shrug of the shoulders and the comment, 'Well, that's just the way it is' is a frequent response to learners' queries. Learners who have had a thorough dose of traditional grammar in their classrooms often do better at answering the question *why?* even though they run the risk of reiterating some oversimplifications inevitable in the pedagogical grammars they are familiar with.

References

Abbott, G. (1983) El otro Lado – or come back, Robert, nearly all is forgiven. *World Language English* 2, 93–96.

Ahukanna, K., Lund, N. and Gentile, J. (1981) Inter- and intralingual interference effects in learning a third language. *Modern Language Journal* 65, 281–287.

Aitchison, J. (1976) *The Articulate Mammal: An Introduction to Psycholinguistics.* London: Hutchinson.

Alanen, R. (1997) Grammaticality judgments and reaction time measurement: A tool for analyzing the use of second language knowledge. PhD dissertation, Jyväskylä University. On WWW at http://selene.lib.jyu.fi: 8080/gradu/f/ alanen.pdf. Accessed 21.07.06.

Albert, M.L. and Obler, L.K. (1978) *The Bilingual Brain: Neuropsychological and Neurolinguistic Aspects of Bilingualism.* New York: Academic Press.

Andersen, R. (1983) Transfer to somewhere. In S. Gass and L. Selinker (eds) *Language Transfer in Language Learning* (pp. 177–201). Rowley, MA: Newbury House.

Andersen, R. (1984) The one-to-one principle of interlanguage construction. *Language Learning* 34, 77–95.

Anderson, J.R. (1983) *The Architecture of Cognition.* Cambridge, MA: Harvard UP.

Anderson, J.R. and Lebriere, C. (1998) *The Atomic Components of Thought.* Mahwah, NJ: Lawrence Erlbaum Associates.

Arabski, J. (1979) *Errors as Indications of the Development of Interlanguage.* Katowice: Uniwersytet Slasky.

Ard, J. and Homburg, T. (1983) Verification of language transfer. In S. Gass and L. Selinker (eds) *Language Transfer in Language Learning* (pp. 157–176). Rowley, MA: Newbury House.

Asher, J.J. (1977) *Learning Another Language through Actions: The Complete Teacher's Guidebook.* Los Gatos, CA: Sky Oaks Productions.

Ausubel, D.P. (1968) *Educational Psychology: A Cognitive View.* New York: Holt, Rinehart and Winston.

Back, H. (1992) A comparative study of the proficiency in English of Finnish and Swedish students at university level. Unpublished MA thesis, Åbo Akademi University.

Bahns, J. and Eldaw, M. (1993) Should we teach EFL students collocations? *System* 21, 101–114.

Banta, F.G. (1981) Teaching German vocabulary: The use of English cognates and common loanwords. *Modern Language Journal* 65, 129–136.

Bartelt, H.G. (1983) Transfer and variability of rhetorical redundancy in Apachean English interlanguage. In S. Gass and L. Selinker (eds) *Language Transfer in Language Learning* (pp. 297–305). Rowley, MA: Newbury House.

Bentahila, A. (1975) The influence of L2 on the learning of L3. Unpublished MA dissertation, University College of North Wales, Bangor.

Bergh, G. (1986) *The Neuropsychological Status of Swedish–English Subsidiary Bilinguals.* Gothenburg Studies in English 61. Gothenburg University.

Berman, R. and Slobin, D. (eds) (1994) *Relating Events in Narrative: A Crosslinguistic Developmental Study.* Hillsdale, NJ: Lawrence Erlbaum.

Biskup, D. (1992) L1 influence on learners' renderings of English collocations: A Polish/German empirical study. In P.J.L. Arnaud and H. Bejoint (eds) *Vocabulary and Applied Linguistics* (pp. 85–93). London: Macmillan.

Björklund, S. and Suni, I. (2000) The role of English as L3 in a Swedish immersion programme in Finland: Impacts on language teaching and language relations. In J. Cenoz and U. Jessner (eds) *English in Europe: The Acquisition of a Third Language* (pp. 198–221). Clevedon: Multilingual Matters.

Bonnet, G. (ed.) (2004) *The Assessment of Pupils' Skills in English in Eight European Countries 2002: A European Project.* Commissioned by The European Network of Policy Makers for the Evaluation of Education Systems. On WWW at http://cisad.adc.education.fr/reva/. Accessed 21.07.06.

Briére, E.J. (1966) An investigation of phonological interference. *Language* 42, 768–796.

Broselow, E. (1984) An investigation of transfer in second language phonology. *International Review of Applied Linguistics* 22, 253–269.

Brown, C. and Payne, M. (1994) Five essential steps of processes in vocabulary learning. Paper presented at the TESOL Convention, Baltimore, MD.

Brown, T. and Haynes, M. (1985) Literacy background and reading development in a second language. In T.H. Carr (ed.) *The Development of Reading Skills* (pp. 19–34). San Francisco, CA: Jossey-Bass.

Cenoz, J. (2001) The effect of linguistic distance, L2 status and age on cross-linguistic influence in third language acquisition. In J. Cenoz, B. Hufeisen and U. Jessner (eds) *Cross-linguistic Influence in Third Language Acquisition* (pp. 8–20). Clevedon: Multilingual Matters.

Cenoz, J., Hufeisen, B. and Jessner, U. (eds) (2001) *Cross-linguistic Influence in Third Language Acquisition.* Clevedon: Multilingual Matters.

Cenoz, J., Hufeisen, B. and Jessner, U. (eds) (2003) *The Multilingual Lexicon.* Dordrecht: Kluwer.

Cenoz, J. and Jessner, U. (eds) (2000) *English in Europe: The Acquisition of a Third Language.* Clevedon: Multilingual Matters.

Chafe, W.L. (1980) *The Pear Stories: Cognitive, Cultural and Linguistic Aspects of Narrative Production.* Norwood, NJ: Ablex.

Chamot, A.U. and Rubin, J. (1994) Comments on Janie Rees-Miller's 'A critical appraisal of learner training: Theoretical bases and teaching implications'. *TESOL Quarterly* 28, 771–776.

Channell, J. (1988) Psycholinguistic considerations in the study of L2 vocabulary acquisition. In R. Carter and M. McCarthy (eds) *Vocabulary and Language Teaching* (pp. 83–96). London: Longman.

Chumbow, B.S. (1981) The mother tongue hypothesis in a multilingual setting. In J-G. Savard and L. Laforge (eds) *Proceedings of the 5th AILA Congress in Montreal 1978* (pp. 42–55). Quebec: Les Presses del' Université de Laval.

Clark, E.C. (1993) *The Lexicon in Acquisition.* Cambridge: Cambridge University Press.

Clark, E.C. and Hecht, B.F. (1983) Comprehension, production and language acquisition. *Annual Review of Psychology* 34, 325–349.

Clyne, M. (1997) Some of the things trilinguals do. *International Journal of Bilingualism* 1, 95–116.

Clyne, M. and Cassia, P. (1999) Trilingualism, immigration and relatedness of languages. International Review of Applied Linguistics 123–124, 57–74.

Clyne, M., Hunt, C.R. and Isaakidis, T. (2004) Learning a community language as a third language. *International Journal of Multilingualism* 1, 33–52.

Cobb, T. (2003) Analyzing late interlanguage with learner corpora: Quebec replications of three European studies. *Canadian Modern Language Review* 59, 393–423.

Connor, U. (1987) Argumentative patterns in student essays: Cross-cultural differences. In U. Connor and R.B. Kaplan (eds) *Writing across Languages: Analysis of L2 Text* (pp. 57–71). Reading, MA: Addison-Wesley.

Connor, U. (1996) *Contrastive Rhetoric: Cross-cultural Aspects of Second Language Writing.* Cambridge: Cambridge University Press.

Corder, S.P. (1967) The significance of learners' errors. *International Review of Applied Linguistics* 5, 161–169.

Corder, S.P. (1973) *Introducing Applied Linguistics.* Harmondsworth: Penguin.

Corder, S.P. (1977) Language continua and the interlanguage hypothesis. In S.P. Corder and E. Roulet (eds) *The Notions of Simplification, Interlanguage and Pidgins and their Relations to Second Language Pedagogy* (pp. 11–17). Neuchatel: Université de Neuchatel.

Corder, S.P. (1979) Language distance and the magnitude of the language learning task. *Studies in Second Language Acquisition* 2, 27–36.

Corder, S.P. (1983) A role for the mother tongue. In S. Gass and L. Selinker (eds) *Language Transfer in Language Learning* (pp. 85–97). Rowley, MA: Newbury House.

Cornell, A. (1999) Idioms: An approach to identifying major pitfalls for learners. *International Review of Applied Linguistics* 37, 1–22.

Crismore, A., Markkanen, R. and Steffensen, M.A. (1993) Metadiscourse in persuasive writing: A study of texts written by American and Finnish university students. *Written Communication* 10, 39–71.

Cruttenden, A. (1981) Item-learning and system-learning. *Journal of Psycholinguistic Research* 10, 79–88.

Cummins, J. (1978) Bilingualism and the development of metalinguistic awareness. *Journal of Cross-cultural Psychology* 9, 131–148.

Dagut, M.B. (1977) Incongruities in lexical gridding. *International Review of Applied Linguistics* 15, 221–229.

Dagut, M.B. and Laufer, B. (1985) Avoidance of phrasal verbs by English learners, speakers of Hebrew: A case for contrastive analysis. *Studies in Second Language Acquisition* 7, 73–79.

Dahlin, H-L. (2001) On the role of lexical transfer in third language acquisition and production. Unpublished MA thesis, Åbo Akademi University.

Daulton, F.E. (2004) *Gairaigo:* The built-in lexicon? The common loanwords in Japanese based on high-frequency English vocabulary and their effect on language acquisition. Unpublished PhD dissertation, Victoria University of Wellington.

Davies, A. (1994) Proficiency or the native speaker: What are we trying to achieve in ELT? In G. Cook and B. Seidlhofer (eds) *Principle and Practice in Applied Linguistics* (pp. 145–157). Oxford: Oxford University Press.

Davies, N.F. (1978) *Putting Receptive Skills First: An Investigation into Sequencing in Modern Language Learning*. Linköping University, Department of Language and Literature.

De Angelis, G. (2001) Interlanguage influence and multilingualism: An empirical investigation into typologically similar and dissimilar languages. Unpublished PhD dissertation, Birkbeck College, University of London.

De Angelis, G. (2005) Interlanguage transfer of function words. *Language Learning* 55, 379–414.

De Bot, K. (2004) The multilingual lexicon: Modelling selection and control. *International Journal of Multilingualism* 1, 17–32.

Dechert, H.W. and Raupach, M. (eds) (1989) *Transfer in Language Production*. Norwood, NJ: Ablex.

DeKeyser, R. (2003) Implicit and explicit learning. In C. Doughty and M. Long (eds) *The Handbook of Second Language Acquisition* (pp. 313–348). Oxford: Blackwell.

DeKeyser, R. (2005) Proceduralisation: The bottleneck in second language skill development. Paper given at the University of Maryland at College Park, December 7.

Denninghaus, F. (1976) Der kontrollierte Erwerb eines potentiellen Wortschatzes im Fremdsprachenunterricht. *Praxis des neusprachlichen Unterrichts* 23, 3–14.

Dewaele, J-M. (1998) Lexical inventions: French interlanguage as L2 versus L3. *Applied Linguistics* 19, 471–490.

Dörnyei, Z. and Skehan, P. (2004) Individual differences in second language learning. In C. Doughty and M. Long (eds) *The Handbook of Second Language Acquisition* (pp. 589–630). Oxford: Blackwell.

Duke, J., Hufeisen, B. and Lutjeharms, M. (2004) Die sieben Siebe des EuroCom für den multilingualen Einstieg in die Welt der germanischen Sprachen. In H.G. Klein and D. Rutke (eds) *Neuere Forschungen zur Europäischen Interkomprehension* (pp. 109–134). Aachen: Shaker Verlag.

Dulay, H. and Burt, M. (1974) Natural sequences in child second language acquisition. *Language Learning* 24, 37–53.

Dulay, H., Burt, M. and Krashen, S. (eds) (1982) *Language Two*. New York: Oxford University Press.

Duskova, L. (1969) On sources of errors in foreign language learning. *International Review of Applied Linguistics* 7, 11–31.

Duskova, L. (1984) Similarity: An aid or hindrance in foreign language learning? *Folia Linguistica* 18, 103–115.

Eckman, F.R. (1981) On predicting phonological difficulty in second language acquisition. *Studies in Second Language Acquisition* 4, 18–30.

Eckman, F.R. (1996) On evaluating arguments for special nativism in second language acquisition theory. *Second Language Research* 12, 398–419.

Eckman, F.R. (ed.) (1996) Special issue on general nativism and second language acquisition. *Second Language Research* 12, 4.

Eckman, F.R. (2004) From phonemic differences to constraint rankings: Research on second language phonology. *Studies in Second Language Acquisition* 26, 513–549.

Ek, M. and Tani, B. (1985) Bilingualism and the learning of a third language: A test in English with commercial college students. Unpublished MA thesis, Åbo Akademi University.

Ekblom, E. (1933) *Skenbar och verklig betydelse i engelskan*. Stockholm: Norstedt.

Ekholm, G. (1987) The role of a language learner's mother tongue: A study of transfer among Swedish- and Finnish-speaking primary school pupils. Unpublished MA thesis, Åbo Akademi University.

Elert, C-C. (ed.) (1981) *Internordisk språkförståelse. Umeå Studies in the Humanities* 33. Umeå: Umeå University.

Ellegård, A. (1978) On measuring language similarity. In J. Weinstock (ed.) *Nordic Languages and Linguistics* (pp. 195–216). University of Texas.

Ellis, N. (1997) Vocabulary acquisition: Word structure, collocation, word-class and meaning. In N. Schmitt and M. McCarthy (eds) *Vocabulary: Description, Acquisition and Pedagogy* (pp. 122–139). Cambridge: Cambridge University Press.

Ellis, R. (1985) *Understanding Second Language Acquisition.* Oxford: Oxford University Press.

Ellis, R. (1995) *The Study of Second Language Acquisition.* Oxford: Oxford University Press.

Ellis, R. (1999) Item learning vs. system learning: Exploring free variation. *Applied Linguistics* 20, 460–480.

Elo, A. (1993) Le Francais parlé par les étudiants finnophones et suedophones. PhD dissertation, University of Turku.

Engberg, M. (1993) Receptive vocabulary knowledge in students of English at Åbo Akademi. Unpublished MA thesis, Åbo Akademi University.

Enkvist, N.E. (1973) Should we count errors or measure success? In J. Svartvik (ed.) *Errata: Papers in Error Analysis* (pp. 16–23). Lund: CWK Gleerup.

Ernolv, C. (1958) False friends: Förrädiska ord. *Moderna språk* 52, 347–368.

Ervin, S. (1961) Changes with age in the verbal determinants of word association. *American Journal of Psychology* 74, 361–372.

Eubank, L. and Schwartz, B. (eds) (1996) Special issue on the L2 initial state. *Second Language Research* 12: 1.

European Network. Website at http://cisad.adc.education.fr/reva/pdf/assessment ofenglish.pdf. Accessed 21.07.06.

Faerch, C., Haastrup, K. and Phillipson, R. (1984) *Learner Language and Language Learning.* Clevedon: Multilingual Matters.

Faerch, C. and Kasper, G. (1987) Perspectives on language transfer. *Applied Linguistics* 8, 111–136.

Fay, D. and Cutler, A. (1977) Malapropisms and the structure of the mental lexicon. *Linguistic Inquiry* 8, 505–520.

Flynn, S. (1986) Production vs. comprehension: Differences in underlying competencies. *Studies in Second Language Acquisition* 8, 135–164.

Forsman, L. (2004) Language, culture, and context: Exploring knowledge and attitudes among Finland-Swedish EFL students with particular focus on extracurricular influence. *Report No 7.* Vasa: Åbo Akademi University Faculty of Education.

Galanter, E. (1966) *Textbook of Elementary Psychology.* San Francisco, CA: Holden Day.

Garnham, A. (1985) *Psycholinguistics: Central Topics.* London: Methuen.

Gass, S. (1996) The role of language transfer. In W.C. Ritchie and T.K. Bhatia (eds) *Handbook of Second Language Acquisition* (pp. 317–345). San Diego, CA: Academic Press.

Gass, S. and Selinker, L. (eds) (1983) *Language Transfer in Language Learning.* Rowley, MA: Newbury House.

George, H.V. (1972) *Common Errors in Language Learning.* Rowley, MA: Newbury House.

Gibson, M. and Hufeisen, B. (2003) Investigating the role of prior foreign language knowledge. In J. Cenoz, B. Hufeisen and U. Jessner (eds) *The Multilingual Lexicon* (pp. 87–102). Dordrecht: Kluwer.

Gociman, A. and Bantas, A. (1976) Whence the English deceptive cognates. In D. Chitoran (ed.) *Second International Conference on English Contrastive Projects* (pp. 317–323). Bucharest.

Granbacka, S. (1985) Apologising in English, Swedish and Finnish: A contrastive study with special reference to communicative competence. Unpublished MA thesis, Åbo Akademi University.

Granfors, T. and Palmberg, R. (1976). Errors made by Finns and Swedish-speaking Finns learning English at a commercial-college level. In H. Ringbom and R. Palmberg (eds) Errors made by Finns and Swedish-speaking Finns in the learning of English: Working papers by members of the error-analysis project (pp.14–53). Department of English, Åbo Akademi.

Granger, S. (1993) Cognates: An aid or a barrier to successful L2 vocabulary development. *ITL Review of Applied Linguistics* 99–100, 43–56.

Granger, S. (1996) Romance words in English: From history to pedagogy. In J. Svartvik (ed.) *Words* (pp. 105–121). Proceedings of an International Symposium, Lund, 25–26 August. Organised under the auspices of the Royal Academy of Letters, History and Antiquities and sponsored by the Foundation Natur och Kultur Publishers. Stockholm.

Granger, S. (ed.) (1998) *Learner English on Computer.* London: Longman.

Haastrup, K. (1991) *Lexical Inferencing Procedures or Talking about Words: A Book about Receptive Procedures in Foreign Language Learning with Special Reference to English.* Tübingen: Gunter Narr.

Haastrup, K. and Henriksen, B. (2000) Vocabulary acquisition: Acquiring depth of knowledge through network building. *International Journal of Applied Linguistics* 10, 221–239.

Håkansson, G. (1994) Typological markedness in action in the classroom: Some observations on the acquisition of German in Swedish schools. Paper presented at the EUROSLA conference in Aix-en-Provence, September.

Hall, C.J. (2002) The automatic cognate form assumption: Evidence for the parasitic model of vocabulary development. *International Review of Applied Linguistics* 40, 69–87.

Hall, C.J. and Ecke, P. (2005) Language typology and form–frame interaction in the multilingual mental lexicon: Evidence from L3 German and L3 French learners. Unpublished paper, Fourth International Conference on L3 Acquisition and Multilingualism in Fribourg, September.

Hammarberg, B. (1974) The insufficiency of error analysis. *International Review of Applied Linguistics* 12, 185–192.

Hammarberg, B. (2001) Roles of L1 and L2 in L3 production and acquisition. In J. Cenoz, B. Hufeisen and U. Jessner (eds) *Cross-linguistic Influence in Third Language Acquisition* (pp. 21–41). Clevedon: Multilingual Matters.

Hammarberg, B. and Williams, S. (1993) A study of third language acquisition. In B. Hammarberg (ed.) *Problem, Process, Product in Language Learning* (pp. 60–70). Stockholm University, Department of Linguistics.

Hammer, P. and Giauque, G.S. (1989) *The Role of Cognates in the Teaching of French*. New York: Peter Lang.

Hammer, P. and Monod, M. (1976) *English–French Cognate Dictionary*. Edmonton, Alberta: University of Alberta.

Hammer, P. and Monod, M. (1978) The role of French–English cognates in listening comprehension. *Audio-Visual Language Journal* 16, 29–32.

Hammerly, H. (1991) *Fluency and Accuracy*. Clevedon: Multilingual Matters.

Hargevik, S. and Stevens, M. (1978) *English Synonyms and False Friends*. Lund: Liber läromedel.

Harley, B. (1995) Introduction: The lexicon in second language research. In B. Harley (ed.) *Lexical Issues in Language Learning* (pp. 1–28). Ann Arbor: John Benjamins.

Harley, B., Hart, D. and Lapkin, S. (1986) *The Effects of Early Bilingual Schooling on First Language Skills*. Cambridge: Cambridge University Press.

Hasselgren, A. (1994) Lexical teddy bears and advanced learners: A study into the ways Norwegian students cope with English vocabulary. *International Journal of Applied Linguistics* 4, 237–260.

Hatch, E. and Brown, C. (1995) *Vocabulary, Semantics, and Language Education*. Cambridge: Cambridge University Press.

Hedquist, R. (1985) Nederländares förståelse av danska och svenska. *Rapport 3*. Umeå: Umeå universitet, Institutionerna för fonetik och nordiska språk.

Heikkinen, H. and Valo, M. (1984) Slips in interaction: The psychopathology of everyday interaction. *Jyväsiä 1984 Papers and Reports*. Jyväskylä: Dept. of Applied Linguistics and Speech (Also published in J.P. Forgas (ed.) *Language and Social Situations*. New York: Springer.)

Henning, G.H. (1973) Remembering foreign language vocabulary: Acoustic and semantic parameters. *Language Learning* 23, 185–196.

Henriksen, B. (1999) Three dimensions of vocabulary development. *Studies in Second Language Acquisition* 21, 303–317.

Henriksen, B. and Haastrup, K. (1998) Describing learners' lexical competence across tasks and over time: A focus on research design. In K. Haastrup and Å. Viberg (eds) *Perspectives on Lexical Acquisition in a Second Language: Travaux de l'Institute de Linguistique de Lund* 38 (pp. 61–95). Lund: Lund University Press.

Herranen, T. (1978) Errors made by Finnish university students in the use of the English article system. In K. Sajavaara, J. Lehtonen and R. Markkanen (eds) *Further Contrastive Papers. Jyväskylä Contrastive Studies* 6, 74–95.

Huckin, T. and Coady, J. (1999) Incidental vocabulary acquisition in a second language: A review. *Studies in Second Language Acquisition* 21, 181–193.

Hufeisen, B. (2005) Mehrsprachigkeit: Fit für Babel. *Gehirn & Geist. Das Magazin für Psychologie und Hirnforschung* 6, 28–33.

Hurskainen, A. (2000) *Swahilin peruskurssi (Introduction to Swahili)*. Helsinki.

Ijaz, I.H. (1986) Linguistic and cognitive determinants of lexical acquisition in a second language. *Language Learning* 36, 401–451.

Ingberg, M. (1987) Finland-Swedish paragraph patterns in EFL student composi- tions. In I. Lindblad and M. Ljung (eds) *Proceedings from the Third Nordic Confer- ence for English Studies* (Vol. II). *Stockholm Studies in English* 74: 417–426. Stockholm: Almqvist & Wiksell.

Ingram, D. (1974) The relationship between comprehension and production. In R.L. Schiefelbusch and L.L. Lloyd (eds) *Language Perspectives: Acquisition, Retardation and Intervention* (pp. 313–334). London: Macmillan.

Ingram, E. (1975) Psychology and language learning. In J.B.P. Allen and S.P. Corder (eds) *Papers in Applied Linguistics. The Edinburgh Course in Applied Linguistics* (Vol. 2; pp. 218–290). London: Oxford University Press.

INS (2004) Internordisk språkförståelse i en tid med ökad internationalisering 2003–2004. Unpublished paper, INS-projektet Lunds Universitet.

Isaksson-Wikberg, M. (1999) *Negotiated and Committed Argumentation: A Cross-cultural Study of American and Finland-Swedish Student Writing*. Åbo: Åbo Akademi University Press.

Ivir, V. (1968) Serbo-Croat–English false pair types. *Studia Romanica et Anglica Zagrebiensia* 25–26, 149–159.

James, C. (1980) *Contrastive Analysis*. London: Longman.

James, C. (1991) The 'Monitor Model' and the role of the first language. In V. Ivir and D. Kalogjera (eds) *Languages in Contact and Contrast: Essays in Contact Linguistics to Honour Rudolf Filipovic* (pp. 249–260). The Hague: Mouton.

James, C. (1993) 'Don't shoot my dodo!' Keynote paper at the 10th AILACongress, Amsterdam.

James, C. (1998) *Errors in Language Learning and Use: Exploring Error Analysis*. London: Longman.

Järviaho, M. (2004) Transfer in the lexis of third language learners: A study of ninth form learners of English in two comprehensive schools in Finland. Unpublished MA thesis, Åbo Akademi University.

Jarvis, S. (1997) The role of L1-based concepts in L2 lexical reference. PhD dissertation, Indiana University.

Jarvis, S. (2000) Methodological rigor in the study of transfer. *Language Learning* 50, 245–309.

Jarvis, S. and Odlin, T. (2000) Morphological type, spatial reference, and language transfer. *Studies in Second Language Acquisition* 22, 535–556.

Jarvis, S. and Pavlenko, A. (in press) *Crosslinguistic Influence on Language and Cognition*. Mahwah, NJ: Lawrence Erlbaum.

Jessner, U. (1999) Metalinguistic awareness in multilinguals: Cognitive aspects of third language learning. *Language Awareness* 8, 201–209.

Jessner, U. (2003) The nature of cross-linguistic interaction in the multilingual system. In J. Cenoz, B. Hufeisen and U. Jessner (eds) *The Multilingual Lexicon* (pp. 45–55). Dordrecht: Kluwer.

Joannopoulou, M. (2002) Form and meaning in the second language lexicon. *Journal of Applied Linguistics* 18, 29–42.

Johnson, K. (1996) *Language Teaching and Skill Learning*. Oxford: Blackwell.

Juhász, J. (1970) *Probleme der Interferenz*. München: Max Hueber.

Kaplan, R.B. (1966) Cultural thought patterns in intercultural education. *Language Learning* 16, 1–20.

Karlsson, F. (1977) Morphotactic structure and word cohesion in Finnish. In K. Sajavaara and J. Lehtonen (eds) *Contrastive Papers. Jyväskylä Contrastive Studies* 4, 59–74. University of Jyväskylä.

Kasper, G. and Rose, K.R. (2002) *Pragmatic Development in a Second Language. Language Learning* (Vol. 52, Supplement 1). University of Michigan: Blackwell.

Kellerman, E. (1977) Towards a characterisation of the strategy of transfer in second language learning. *Interlanguage Studies Bulletin, Utrecht* 2, 58–145.

Kellerman, E. (1978) Giving learners a break: Native language intuitions as a source of predictions about transferability. *Working Papers on Bilingualism* 15, 59–92.

Kellerman, E. (1984) The empirical evidence for the influence of the L1 in interlanguage. In A. Davies, C. Criper and A.P.R. Howatt (eds) *Interlanguage* (pp. 98–122). Edinburgh: Edinburgh University Press.

Kellerman, E. (1995) Crosslinguistic influence: Transfer to nowhere? *Annual Review of Applied Linguistics* 15, 125–150.

Kellerman, E. (2001) New uses for old language: Cross-linguistic and cross-gestural influence in the narratives of non-native speakers. In J. Cenoz, B. Hufeisen and U. Jessner (eds) *Cross-linguistic Influence in Third Language Acquisition* (pp. 170–191). Clevedon: Multilingual Matters.

Kellerman, E. and Sharwood Smith, M. (eds) (1986) *Crosslinguistic Influence in Second Language Acquisition*. Language Teaching Methodology Series. Oxford: Pergamon Press.

Kirsner, K., Lalor, E. and Hird, K. (1993) The bilingual lexicon: Exercise, meaning and morphology. In R. Schreuder and B. Weltens (eds) *The Bilingual Lexicon* (pp. 215–248). Amsterdam: John Benjamins.

Klein, H.G. (2002) Current state of development of Eurocomprehension research. On WWW at http://www.eurocomresearch.net/lit/Klein%20EN.htm. Last accessed 21.07.06.

Klein, H.G. and Stegmann, T.D. (2000) *EuroComRom: Die sieben Siebe: Romanische Sprachen sofort lesen können*. Aachen: Shaker.

Kleinmann, H.H. (1977) Avoidance in adult second language acquisition. *Language Learning* 27, 93–107.

Koda, K. (1997) Orthographic knowledge in L2 lexical processing: A cross-linguistic perspective. In J. Coady and T. Huckin (eds) *Second Language Vocabulary Acquisition* (pp. 35–54). Cambridge: Cambridge University Press.

Kolers, P. (1966) Reading and talking bilingually. *American Journal of Psychology* 79, 357–376.

Koster, C.J. (1987) *Word Recognition in Foreign and Native Language*. Dordrecht: Foris Publications.

Kotsinas, U-B. (1983) On the acquisition of vocabulary in immigrant Swedish. In H. Ringbom (ed.) *Psycholinguistics and Foreign Language Learning* (pp. 75–100). Publications of the Research Institute of the Åbo Akademi Foundation 86. Åbo: Åbo Akademi.

Krashen, S. (1985) *The Input Hypothesis: Issues and Implications*. London: Longman.

Kroll, J. and de Groot, A. (1997) Lexical and conceptual memory in the bilingual: Mapping form to meaning in two languages. In A. de Groot and J. Kroll (eds) *Tutorials in Bilingualism. Psychological Perspectives* (pp. 169–199). Mahwah, NJ: Lawrence Erlbaum.

Kroll, J. and Dijkstra, T. (2002) The bilingual lexicon. In R.B. Kaplan (ed.) *The Oxford Handbook of Applied Linguistics* (pp. 301–321). Oxford: Oxford University Press.

Lado, R. (1957) *Linguistics across Cultures: Applied Linguistics for Language Teachers*. Ann Arbor, MI: University of Michigan Press.

Laitakari, K. (2001) Skillnader mellan L1 och L2 vid inlärningen av ett tredje språk: En komparation av finsk och engelsk transfer i inlärarsvenska. Unpublished MA thesis, Åbo Akademi University.

Lasagabaster, D. (2000) Three languages and three linguistic models in the Basque educational system. In J. Cenoz and U. Jessner (eds) *English in Europe: The Acquisition of a Third Language* (pp. 179–197). Clevedon: Multilingual Matters.

Laufer, B. (1988) The concept of 'synforms' (similar lexical forms) in vocabulary acquisition. *Language and Education* 2, 113–132.

Laufer, B. (1990) Words you know: How they affect the words you learn. In J. Fisiak (ed.) *Further Insights in Contrastive Linguistics* (pp. 573–593). Amsterdam: John Benjamins.

Laufer, B. (1991) The development of lexis. *Modern Language Journal* 75, 440–448.

Laufer, B. (1997) What's in a word that makes it hard or easy: Some intralexical factors that affect the learning of words. In N. Schmitt and M. McCarthy (eds) *Vocabulary: Description, Acquisition and Pedagogy* (pp. 140–155). Cambridge: Cambridge University Press.

Laufer, B. and Eliasson, S. (1993) What causes avoidance in L2 learning, L1–L2 difference, L1–L2 similarity or L2 complexity? *Studies in Second Language Acquisition* 15, 35–48.

Lehtonen, J. (1979) Speech rate and pauses in the English of Finns, Swedish-speaking Finns, and Swedes. In R. Palmberg (ed.) *Perception and Production of English: Papers on Interlanguage.* AFTIL (Vol. 6; pp. 35–75). Department of English, Åbo Akademi.

Lehtonen, J. (1981) Psykolingvistiska aspekter på en finnes förmåga att förstå skandinaviska språk. In C-C. Elert and A. Seppänen (eds) *Finnish–English Language Contact: Papers from a Workshop* (pp. 5–22). *Umeå Papers in English 4.* Umeå: Umeå University.

Lehtonen, J. (2002) *Samspel och kommunikation.* Jyväskylä universitet, Institutionen för kommunikationsvetenskaper.

Lehtonen, J. Sajavaara, K. and Manninen, S. (1985) Communication apprehension and attitudes towards a foreign language. *Scandinavian Working Papers on Bilingualism* 5, 53–62.

Lesniewska, J. (2006) Is cross-linguistic influence a factor in advanced EFL learners' use of collocations? In J. Arabski (ed.) *Cross-linguistic Influences in the Second Language Lexicon* (pp. 65–77). Clevedon: Multilingual Matters.

Levelt, W.J.M. (1975) Systems, skills and language learning. In A.L. van Essen and J.P. Menting (eds) *The Context of Foreign-Language Learning* (pp. 83–99). Assen: Van Gorcum.

Levelt, W.J.M. (1977) Skill theory and language teaching. *Studies in Second Language Acquisition* 1, 53–70.

Levenston, E. (1971) Over-indulgence and under-representation: Aspects of mother tongue interference. In G. Nickel (ed.) *Contrastive Linguistics* (pp. 115–121). London: Cambridge University Press.

Levenston, E. (1979) Second language acquisition: Issues and problems. *Interlanguage Studies Bulletin, Utrecht* 4, 147–160.

Lewis, G. and Massad, C.E. (1975) *The Teaching of English as a Foreign Language in Ten Countries.* Stockholm: Almqvist & Wiksell.

Lightbown, P. and Libben, G. (1984) The recognition and use of cognates by L2 learners. In R.W. Andersen (ed.) *A Cross-linguistic Perspective for Second Language Research* (pp. 393–417). Rowley, MA: Newbury House.

Lindros, R. (1987) Communication apprehension in Finland-Swedes speaking English: A contrastive study of self-evaluating results. Unpublished MA thesis, Åbo Akademi University.

Linnakylä, P. and Saari, H. (eds) (1993) *Oppiiko oppilas peruskoulussa? (Do Students Learn in Comprehensive school?).* Jyväskylä: The Institute for Educational Research.

Linnakylä, P. and Välijärvi, J. (2003) Finnish students' performance in PISA: Why such a success? On WWW at http://www.oph.fi/info/finlandinpisastudies/conference2005/jounivalijarvi.doc. Accessed 22.07.06. (Published in German in D. Hänisch and R. Schwalbach (eds) *Forum Jugendarbeit International* (pp. 284–295). Bonn: Internationaler Jugendaustausch- und Besucherdienst der Bundesrepublik Deutschland.)

Lorch, M. P. and Meara, P. (1989) How people listen to languages they don't know. *Language Sciences* 11, 343–353.

Lotto, L. and de Groot, A.M.B. (1998) Effects of learning method and word type on acquiring vocabulary in an unfamiliar language. *Language Learning* 58, 31–69.

Lowie, W. and Verspoor, M. (2004) Input versus transfer? The role of frequency and similarity in the acquisition of L2 prepositions. In M. Achard and S. Niemeier (eds) *Cognitive Linguistics, Second Language Acquisition and Foreign Language Teaching* (pp. 77–94). Berlin: Mouton de Gruyter.

Lübke, D. (1984) Der potentielle Wortschatz in Französisch. *Praxis des neusprachlichen Unterrichts* 31, 372–379.

Mackey, W.F. (1965) *Language Teaching Analysis.* London: Longman.

Maeshiba, N., Yoshinaga, N., Kasper, G. and Ross, S. (1996) Transfer and proficiency in interlanguage apologising. In S.M. Gass and J. Neu (eds) *Speech Acts across Cultures: Challenges to Communication in a Second Language* (pp. 155–187). Berlin: Mouton de Gruyter.

Mägiste, E. (1984) Learning a third language. *Journal of Multilingual and Multicultural Development* 5, 415–421.

Major, R. (1987) A model for interlanguage phonology. In G. Ioup and S. Weinberger (eds) *Interlanguage Phonology: The Acquisition of a Second Language Sound System,* (pp. 101–124). Rowley, MA: Newbury House.

Mäntylä, K. (2004) Idioms and language users: The effect of the characteristics of idioms on their recognition and interpretation by native and non-native speakers of English. PhD thesis, Jyväskylä University.

Marton, W. (1977) Foreign vocabulary learning as problem no. 1 of language teaching at the advanced level. *Interlanguage Studies Bulletin, Utrecht* 2, 33–57.

Marx, N. (2005) Is the training of interlingual comprehension strategies possible? Unpublished paper at the Fourth International Conference on Third Language Acquisition and Multilingualism in Fribourg, September.

Marx, N. and Hufeisen, B. (2004) Review article: Critical overview of research on third language acquisition and multilingualism published in the German language. *International Journal of Multilingualism* 1, 141–154.

Mauranen, A. (1993) *Cultural Differences in Academic Rhetoric.* Frankfurt am Main: Peter Lang.

Maurud, Ö. (1976) Nabospråksforståelse i Skandinavia. *Nordisk utredningsserie NU* 1976: 13.

McAllister, R., Flege, J.E. and Piske, T. (2002) The influence of L1 on the acquisition of Swedish quantity by native speakers of Spanish, English and Estonian. *Journal of Phonetics* 30, 229–258.

McCann, W.J., Klein, H.G. and Stegmann, T.D. (2003) *EuroComRom: The Seven Sieves: How to Read all the Romance Languages Right Away* (2nd revd edn). Aachen: Shaker.

McLaughlin, B. and Nayak, N. (1989) Processing a new language: Does knowing other languages make a difference? In H.W. Dechert and M. Raupach (eds) *Interlingual Processes* (pp. 5–16). Tübingen: Gunter Narr.

Meara, P. (1978) Learners' word associations in French. *Interlanguage Studies Bulletin, Utrecht* 3, 192–211.

Meara, P. (1982) Word association in a foreign language: A report on the Birkbeck vocabulary project. *Nottingham Linguistic Circular* 11, 29–38.

Meara, P. (1988) Learning words in an L1 and an L2. *Polyglot* 9, 1–19.

Meara, P. (1990) A note on passive vocabulary. *Second Language Research* 6, 151–154.

Meara, P. (1993) The bilingual lexicon and the teaching of vocabulary. In R. Schreuder and B. Weltens (eds) *The Bilingual Lexicon* (pp. 279–295). Amsterdam: John Benjamins.

Meara, P. (1995) The importance of an early emphasis on L2 vocabulary. *The Language Teacher* 19, 8–10.

Meara, P. (1997) Towards a new approach to modelling vocabulary acquisition. In N. Schmitt and M. McCarthy (eds) *Vocabulary: Description, Acquisition and Pedagogy* (pp. 109–121). Cambridge: Cambridge University Press.

Meara, P. (no date) Vocabulary profiles. Unpublished paper.

Meissner, F-J. and Burk, H. (2001) Hörverstehen in einer unbekannten romanischen Fremdsprache: Methodische Implikationen für den Tertiärsprachenerwerb. *Zeitschrift für Fremdsprachenforschung* 12, 63–102.

Meissner, F-J. and Reinfried, M. (eds) (1998) *Mehrsprachigkeitsdidaktik: Konzepte, Analysen, Lehrerfahrungen mit romanischen Fremdsprachen*. Tübingen: Gunter Narr.

Melka, F. (1997) Receptive vs. productive aspects of vocabulary. In N. Schmitt and M. McCarthy (eds) *Vocabulary: Description, Acquisition and Pedagogy* (pp. 84–102). Cambridge: Cambridge University Press.

Meriläinen, L. (2006) Lexical transfer errors in the written English of Finnish Upper Secondary School students. Unpublished licentiate thesis, University of Joensuu.

Meunier, F. (1998) Computer tools for the analysis of learner corpora. In S. Granger (ed.) *Learner English on Computer* (pp. 19–37). London: Longman.

Mondria, J-A. and Wit-deBoer, M. (1991) The effects of contextual richness on the guessability and retention of words in a foreign language. *Applied Linguistics* 12, 249–267.

Nation, I.S.P. (1990) *Teaching and Learning Vocabulary.* New York: Newbury House.

Nemser, W. (1971) Approximative systems of foreign language learners. *International Review of Applied Linguistics* 9, 115–123.

Neuner, G. (1992) The role of experience in a content- and comprehension-oriented approach to learning a foreign language. In P.J.L. Arnaud and H. Bejoint (eds) *Vocabulary and Applied Linguistics* (pp. 156–166). London: Macmillan.

Nikula, T. (1996) *Pragmatic Force Modifiers; A Study in Interlanguage Pragmatics.* Jyväskylä: University of Jyväskylä.

Noordman-Vonk, W. (1979) *Retrieval from Semantic Memory.* Berlin: Springer.

Nord, J.R. (1976) Shut up and listen: A case for listening comprehension. Paper presented at the annual national convention of the Association for Educational Communications and Technology, Anaheim, CA (ERIC Document Reproduction Service No. Ed. 122839).

Nurmi, S. (1988) Errors made by Finns and Swedish-speaking Finns in the translation of English in the Matriculation Examination of 1971. Unpublished MA thesis, Åbo Akademi University.

O'Laoire, M. (2004) From L2 to L3/L4: A study of learners' metalinguistic awareness after 13 years of learning Irish. *CLCS Occasional Paper No. 64.* Trinity College, Dublin.

O'Malley, J.M. and Chamot, A.U. (1990) *Learning Strategies in Second Language Acquisition*. Cambridge: Cambridge University Press.
Odlin, T. (1989) *Language Transfer: Cross-linguistic Influence in Language Learning*. Cambridge: Cambridge University Press.
Odlin, T. (2003) Cross-linguistic influence. In C. Doughty and M. Long (eds) *The Handbook of Second Language Acquisition* (pp. 436–486). Oxford: Blackwell.
Odlin, T. and Jarvis, S. (2004) Same source, different outcomes: A study of Swedish influence on the acquisition of English in Finland. *International Journal of Multilingualism* 1, 123–140.
Ohls-Ahlskog, K. (1995) The national test of English 1993 and the English of students in grade 9. Unpublished MA thesis, Åbo Akademi University.
Oller, J.W. (1972) Transfer and interference as special cases of induction and substitution. *Linguistics* 91, 22–33.
Oller, J.W. and Redding, E.Z. (1971) Article usage and other language skills. *Language Learning* 21, 85–95.
Oller, J.W. Jr and Ziahosseiny, S.M. (1970) The contrastive analysis hypothesis and spelling errors. *Language Learning* 20, 183–189.
Påhlsson, C. (1983) Observations on performance in English in Finland. In C-C. Elert and A. Seppänen (eds) *Finnish–English Language Contact: Papers from a Workshop* (pp. 23–71). *Umeå Papers in English* 4. Umeå: Umeå University.
Påhlsson, C. (1999) *Decision-making and Limited Resources: Studies in Interlanguage Vocabulary Space of Learners of English for Special Purposes*. Frankfurt am Main: Peter Lang.
Palmberg, R. (1985) How much English vocabulary do Swedish-speaking primary-school pupils know before starting to learn English at school? In H. Ringbom (ed.) *Foreign Language Learning and Bilingualism. Publications of the Research Institute of the Åbo Akademi Foundation* 105, pp. 89–97.
Palmer, H. (1917/1968) *The Scientific Study and Teaching of Languages*. Language and Language Learning Series. London: Oxford University Press.
Paradis, M. (1985) On the representation of two languages in one brain. *Language Sciences* 7, 1–37.
Paradis, M. (1987) Neurolinguistic perspectives on bilingualism. In M. Paradis and G. Libben (eds) *The Assessment of Bilingual Aphasia* (pp. 1–17). Hillsdale, NJ: Lawrence Erlbaum.
Pavlenko, A. (2000) New approaches to concepts in bilingual memory. *Bilingualism: Language and Cognition* 3, 1–4.
Pavlenko, A. and Jarvis, S. (2002) Bidirectional transfer. *Applied Linguistics* 23, 190–214.
Pienemann, M. (1998) *Language Processing and Second Language Development*. Amsterdam: John Benjamins.
Pietilä, P. (1989) The English of Finnish Americans, with reference to social and psychological background factors and with special reference to age. *Turun yliopiston julkaisuja, Annales Universitatis Turkuensis*, series B, 188.
Pietiläinen, J. (2005) Kielitaito Euroopan Unionissa: Yksinomaan englanti vai monikielinen unioni? (Language proficiency in the European Union: Only English or a multilingual union?) Paper at the AFinLA conference, Turku, November.

Pitkänen, E. (1991) Englanninkielisen sanaston tuntemus suomalaisten peruskoululaisten ja lukiolaisten keskuudessa ennen Englannin kielen kouluopintojen alkamista (The knowledge of English vocabulary by Finnish comprehensive and upper secondary school pupils before the beginning of English studies at school). Internal report. Jyväskylä: Jyväskylän yliopiston monistuskeskus.

Pons-Ridler, S. (1984) Oral comprehension: A new approach. *British Journal of Language Teaching* 22, 87–102.

Postman, L. and Keppel, G. (eds) (1970) *Norms of Word Associations*. New York: Academic Press.

Postovsky, V.A. (1974) Effects of delay in oral practice at the beginning of second language learning. *Modern Language Journal* 58: 5–6, 229–239.

Pressley, M., Levin, J.R. and McDaniel, M.A. (1987) Remembering versus inferring what a word means: Mnemonic and contextual approaches. In M.G. McKeown and M.E.Curtis (ed.) *The Nature of Vocabulary Acquisition* (pp. 107–127). Hillsdale: L. Erlbaum.

Rainio, A-K. (2003) Knowledge of English vocabulary among Finland-Swedish 4th formers: A study conducted in Pargas and Åbo. Unpublished MA thesis, Åbo Akademi University.

Reinfried, M. (1999) Innerromanischer Sprachtransfer. *Grenzgänge. Beiträge zu einer moderner Romanistik* 6 (12), 96–125.

Reves, T and Levine, A. (1988) The foreign language receptive skills: Same or different? *System* 16, 327–336.

Richards, J.C. (1976) The role of vocabulary teaching. *TESOL Quarterly* 10, 77–89.

Ringbom, H. (1978) The influence of the mother tongue on the translation of lexical items. *Interlanguage Studies Bulletin, Utrecht* 3 (1), 80–101.

Ringbom, H. (1987) *The Role of the First Language in Foreign Language Learning*. Clevedon: Multilingual Matters.

Ringbom, H. (1992) On L1 transfer in L2 comprehension and L2 production. *Language Learning* 42, 85–112.

Ringbom, H. (1993) Near-nativeness and the four language skills: Some concluding remarks. In H. Ringbom (ed.) *Near-native Proficiency in English* (pp. 295–306). *English Department Publications* 2. Åbo: Åbo Akademi University.

Ringbom, H. (1995) On English/Swedish false friends. In *Proceedings from the Sixth Nordic Conference for English Studies, Tromsö, May 25–28* (Vol. 2; pp. 471–476). Tromsö: Department of English, University of Tromsö.

Ringbom, H. (1998) Vocabulary frequencies in advanced learner English: A cross-linguistic approach. In S. Granger (ed.) *Learner English on Computer* (pp. 41–52). London: Longman.

Ringbom, H. (2005) L2-transfer in third language acquisition. In B. Hufeisen and R.J. Fouser (eds) *Introductory Readings in L3* (pp. 71–82). Tübingen: Stauffenburg.

Ringbom, H. (2006) The importance of different types of similarity in transfer studies. In J. Arabski (ed.) *Cross-linguistic Influences in the Second Language Lexicon* (pp. 35–45). Clevedon: Multilingual Matters.

Rogers, M. (1997) Language proximity: An applied linguistic perspective. In M. Slodzian and J. Souillot (eds) *Comprehension Multilingue en Europe/Multilingual Comprehension in Europe* (pp. 45–54). Proceedings of the Brussels Seminar 10–11 March. Paris: Centre de Recherche en Ingéniérie Mulitlingue.

Rohlich, C. (2004) Oral-reading miscues of Finnish-Australian informants. In P. Muikku-Werner and H. Stotesbury (eds) *Minä ja Kielitiede. Soveltajan Arki* (pp. 55–71). Jyväskylä: AFinLA Yearbook no 62.

Romaine, S. (2003) Variation. In C. Doughty and M. Long (eds) *The Handbook of Second Language Acquisition* (pp. 409–435). Oxford: Blackwell.

Ryan, A. (1997) Learning the orthographical form of L2 vocabulary: A receptive and a productive process. In N. Schmitt and M. McCarthy (eds) *Vocabulary: Description, Acquisition and Pedagogy* (pp. 181–198). Cambridge: Cambridge University Press.

Ryle, G. (1949) *The Concept of Mind.* London: Hutchinson.

Sajavaara, K. (1983) The article errors of Finnish learners of English. In C-C. Elert and A. Seppänen (eds) *Finnish–English Language Contact: Papers from a Workshop* (pp. 72–87). *Umeå Papers in English* 4. Umeå: Umeå University.

Sajavaara, K. and Lehtonen, J. (1989) Aspects of transfer in foreign language speakers' reactions to acceptability. In H.W. Dechert and M. Raupach (eds) *Interlingual Processes* (pp. 35–52). Tübingen: Gunter Narr.

Sajavaara, K. and Lehtonen, J. (1997) The silent Finn revisited. In A. Jaworski (ed.) *Silence: Interdisciplinary Perspectives* (pp. 263–283). Berlin: Mouton de Gruyter.

Sajavaara, K. and Takala, S. (2000) Kielikoulutuksen vaikutus ja tulokset Suomessa [The effect and results of language education in Finland]. In K. Sajavaara and A. Piirainen-Marsh (eds) *Näkökulmia soveltavaan kielentutkimukseen* [*Aspects of Applied Linguistics*] (pp. 155–230). Jyväskylä: Jyväskylä University.

Sandlund, T. and Björklund, K. (1980) Bilinguals in Finland 1950. Språkgrupp och Mobilitet: Ethnicity and Mobility Research reports. MOB 5. Åbo: Åbo Akademi.

Scarcella, R.C. (1983) Discourse accent in second language performance In S. Gass and L. Selinker (eds) *Language Transfer in Language Learning* (pp. 306–326). Rowley, MA: Newbury House.

Schachter, J. (1983) A new account of language transfer. In S. Gass and L. Selinker (eds) *Language Transfer in Language Learning* (pp. 98–111). Rowley, MA: Newbury House.

Schmidt, R. and Frota, S. (1986) Developing basic conversational ability in a second language: A case study of an adult learner. In R. Day (ed.) *Talking to Learn: Conversation in Second Language Acquisition* (pp. 237–326). Rowley, MA: Newbury House.

Schmitt, N. (1997) Vocabulary learning strategies. In N. Schmitt and M. McCarthy (eds) *Vocabulary: Description, Acquisition and Pedagogy* (pp. 199–227). Cambridge: Cambridge University Press.

Schmitt, N. and McCarthy, M (eds) (1997) *Vocabulary: Description, Acquisition and Pedagogy.* Cambridge: Cambridge University Press.

Schmitt, N. and Meara, P. (1997) Researching vocabulary through a word knowledge framework: Word associations and verbal suffixes. *Studies in Second Language Acquisition* 19, 17–36.

Schouten-van Parreren, C. (1989) Vocabulary learning through reading: Which conditions should be met when presenting words in texts? *AILA Review* 6, 75–85.

Segalowitz, N. (2003) Automaticity and second languages. In C. Doughty and M. Long (eds) *The Handbook of Second Language Acquisition* (pp. 382–408). Oxford: Blackwell.

Selinker, L. (1966) A psycholinguistic study of language transfer. Unpublished PhD dissertation, Georgetown University.

Selinker, L. (1969) Language transfer. *General Linguistics* 9, 67–92.

Selinker, L. (1992) *Rediscovering Interlanguage.* Harlow: Longman.

Selinker, L. and Baumgartner-Cohen, B. (1995) Multiple language acquisition: 'Damn it, why can't I keep these two languages apart?' *Language, Culture and Curriculum* 8, 115–121.

Seppänen, A. (1998) Finnish and English from a comparative perspective. In R.W. Cooper (ed.) *Compare or Contrast: Current Issues in Cross-language Research* (pp. 15–51). *Tampere English Studies* 6. Tampere: Tampere University.

Sharp, D. (1973) *Language in Bilingual Communities. Explorations in Language Study Series.* London: Edward Arnold.

Sharwood Smith, M. (1986) Comprehension versus acquisition: Two ways of processing input. *Applied Linguistics* 7, 239–256.

Sikogukira, M. (1993) Influence of languages other than the L1 on a foreign language: A case of transfer from L2 to L3. *Edinburgh Papers in Applied Linguistics* 5, 110–132.

Singh, R. and Carroll, S. (1979) L1, L2 and L3. *Indian Journal of Applied Linguistics* 5, 51–63.

Singleton, D. (1994) Learning L2 lexis: A matter of form? In G. Bartelt (ed.) *The Dynamics of Language Processes: Essays in Honor of Hans W. Dechert* (pp. 45–57). Tübingen: Gunter Narr.

Singleton, D. (1999) *Exploring the Second Language Mental Lexicon.* Cambridge: Cambridge University Press.

Singleton, D. and Little, D. (1991) The second language lexicon: Some evidence from university-level learners of French and German. *Second Language Research* 7, 61–81.

Singleton, D. and Little, D. (1984/2005) A first encounter with Dutch: Perceived language distance and language transfer as factors in comprehension. In H.W. Dechert and M. Raupach (eds) *Interlingual Processes* (pp. 101–109). Tübingen: Gunter Narr.

Singley, M.K. and Anderson, J.R. (1989) *The Transfer of Cognitive Skill.* Cambridge, MA: Harvard UP.

Sjöholm, K. (1995) *The Influence of Cross-linguistic, Semantic and Input Factors on the Acquisition of English Phrasal Verbs: A Comparison between Finnish and Swedish Learners at an Intermediate and Advanced Level.* Åbo: Åbo Akademi University Press.

Sjöholm, M. (1979) Partial dictation as a testing device: An analysis with special reference to the achievement made by Swedish- and Finnish-speaking applicants for English, 1975. In R. Palmberg (ed.) *Perception and Production of English: Papers on Interlanguage* (pp. 123–166). AFTIL 6. Publications of the Department of English, Åbo Akademi.

Söderman, T. (1993) Word associations of foreign language learners and native speakers. The phenomenon of a shift in response type and its relevance for lexical development. In H. Ringbom (ed.) *Near-native Proficiency in English* (pp. 91–182) *English Department Publications* 2. Åbo: Åbo Akademi University.

Stedje, A. (1977) Tredjespråksinterferens i fritt tal: En jämförande studie. In R. Palmberg and H. Ringbom (eds) *Papers from the Conference on Contrastive Linguistics and Error Analysis 7–8 February. Publications of the Research Institute of the Åbo Akademi Foundation* 19, 141–158.

Stockwell, R. Bowen, J. and Martin, J. (1965) *The Grammatical Structures of English and Spanish.* Chicago: Chicago UP.

Stoye, S. (2000) *Eurocomprehension: Der romanistische Beitrag für eine europäische Mehrsprachigkeit.* Aachen: Shaker.

Strangert, E. and Hedquist, R. (1989) *Hur svenskar uppfattar och förstår nederländska ord.* Rapport 4. Umeå: Umeå universitet, Institutionerna för fonetik och nordiska språk.

Sundqvist, L. (1986) Lexical inferencing among Swedish- and Finnish-speaking primary school pupils. Unpublished MA thesis, Åbo Akademi University.

Suomi, K. (1976) *English Voiceless and Voiced Stops as Produced by Native Finnish Speakers.* Jyväskylä Contrastive Studies 2. Jyväskylä: Jyväskylä University.

Suomi, R. (1984) Spelling errors and interference errors in English made by Finns and Swedish speaking Finns in the 9th form of Comprehensive School. Unpublished MA thesis, Åbo Akademi University.

Swan, M. (1985) A critical look at the communicative approach (2). *English Language Teaching Journal* 39, 76–87.

Swan, M. (1997) The influence of the mother tongue on second language vocabulary acquisition and use. In N. Schmitt and M. McCarthy (eds) *Vocabulary: Description, Acquisition and Pedagogy* (pp. 156–180). Cambridge: Cambridge University Press.

Sweet, H. (1899/1964) *The Practical Study of Languages.* Language and Language Learning Series. London: Oxford University Press.

Takahashi, T. and Beebe, L.M. (1987) The development of pragmatic competence by Japanese learners of English. *JALT Journal* 8, 131–155.

Takala, S. (1984) Evaluation of the students' knowledge of English vocabulary in the Finnish comprehensive school. *Reports from the Institute for Educational Research* 350. Jyväskylä: Jyväskylä University.

Takala, S. (2002) Language planning in the Finnish context: Some observations and arguments. In S. Björklund, M. Koskela and M. Nordman (eds) *Språk som formar vär(l)den: Festskrift till Christer Laurén på 60-årsdagen.* Vaasa: Vaasan yliopiston julkaisuja.

Takala, S. and Havola, L. (1983) English in the socio-linguistic context of Finland. *Institute for Education Research Bulletin* 240. Jyväskylä: Jyväskylä University.

Taylor, I. (1976) Similarity between French and English words: A factor to be considered in bilingual language behaviour? *Journal of Psycholinguistic Research* 5, 85–94.

Tevajärvi, T. (1981) En undersökning av finländares problem vid hörförståelse av danska. In C-C. Elert (ed.) *Internordisk språkförståelse* (pp. 144–164). *Umeå Studies in the Humanities* 33. Umeå: Umeå University.

Thomas, J. (1988) The role played by metalinguistic awareness in second and third language learning. *Journal of Multilingual and Multicultural Development* 9, 235–247.

Thomas, J. (1992) Metalinguistic awareness in second and third language learning. In R.J. Harris (ed.) *Cognitive Processing in Bilinguals* (pp. 531–545). Amsterdam: North Holland.

Trosborg, A. (1987) Apology strategies in natives/non-natives. *Journal of Pragmatics* 11, 147–167.

Tuokko, E. (2000) *Peruskoulun 9.vuosiluokan englannin A1-kieli oppimistulosten kansallinen arviointi 1999.* Oppimistulosten arviointi 3/2000 (A national evaluation of the learning results in English of students in their last year of comprehensive school). Helsinki: Opetushallitus.

Tuokko, E. (2003) *Perusopetuksen päättövaiheen englannin kielen oppimistulosten kansainvälinen arviointi 2002: Suomen tulokse* [*The International Assessment of Pupils' Skills in English in Eight European Countries 2002: The Finnish Results*]. Helsinki: Opetushallitus.

Tyler, A. (1995) The coconstruction of cross-cultural miscommunication: Conflicts in perception, negotiation and enactment of participant role and status. *Studies in Second Language Acquisition* 17, 129–152.

Uchida, E. and Scholfield, P. (2000) Why words differ in difficulty: The learnability of English–Japanese cognates for Japanese learners of English. Paper in preparation: Nov 2000. On WWW at http://privatewww.essex.ac.uk/~scholp/emim art2.htm. Accessed 18.07.06.

Ulijn, J.M., Wolfe, S.J. and Donn, A. (1981) The lexical transfer effect of French knowledge in the acquisition of English by native Vietnamese speakers. Report no. 6: Foreign Language Acquisition Research, THE, Eindhoven University of Technology.

Vaurio, L. (1998) *Lexical Inferencing in Reading English on the Secondary Level.* Jyväskylä: Jyväskylä University.

Vesterlund, B. and Till, I-L (1982) Bilingualism and foreign language learning: An experiment with a cloze test. Unpublished MA thesis, Åbo Akademi University.

Vildomec, V. (1963) *Multilingualism.* Leyden: Sythoff.

Wahlman-Tyrsky, B. (1976) Errors made by Finns and Swedish-speaking Finns in the essays of the entrance test for English at Åbo Akademi 1975. Unpublished MA thesis, Åbo Akademi University.

Waller, T. (1993) Characteristics of near-native proficiency in writing. In H. Ringbom (ed.) *Near-native Proficiency in English* (pp. 183–293). *English Department Publications* 2. Åbo: Åbo Akademi University.

Weinreich, U. (1953/1963) *Languages in Contact: Findings and Problems.* The Hague: Mouton.

Welna, J. (1977) Deceptive words: A study in the contrastive lexicon of Polish and English. *Papers and Studies in Contrastive Linguistics* 7, 73–84.

Werner, K. (1995) Why are some words more difficult to learn than others? A study of Swedish- and Finnish-speaking students' confusions of similar lexical forms in English. Unpublished MA thesis, Åbo Akademi University.

Wesche, M. and Paribakht, S. (1996) Assessing second language vocabulary knowledge: Breadth vs. depth. *Canadian Modern Language Review* 53, 13–39.

Williams, S. and Hammarberg, B. (1998) Language switches in L3 production: Implications for a polyglot speaking model. *Applied Linguistics* 19, 295–333.

Wode, H. (1980) Phonology in L2 acquisition. In S. Felix (ed.) *Second Language Development. Trends and Issues* (pp. 123–136). Tübingen: Gunter Narr.

Wode, H. (1986) Language transfer: A cognitive, functional and developmental view. In E. Kellerman and M. Sharwood Smith, M. (eds) *Crosslinguistic Influence in Second Language Acquisition* (pp. 173–185) *Language Teaching Methodology Series*. Oxford: Pergamon Press.

Yu, L. (1996) The role of L1 in the acquisition of motion verbs in English by Chinese and Japanese learners. *The Canadian Modern Language Review* 53, 191–218.

Zettersten, A. (1979) *Experiments in English Vocabulary Testing. LiberHermods Studies in Language for Special Purposes* (Vol. 1). Malmö: LiberHermods.

Zimmermann, R. (1987) Form-oriented and content-oriented lexical errors in L2 learners. *International Review of Applied Linguistics* 25, 55–67.

Index of Persons Cited